CW01668079

A little course in...

Pilates

A little course in...

Pilates

DK

LONDON, NEW YORK, MELBOURNE, MUNICH, DELHI

Project Editor Becky Shackleton
Project Art Editor Gemma Fletcher
Senior Editor Alastair Laing
Managing Editor Penny Warren
Managing Art Editor Alison Donovan
Senior Jacket Creative Nicola Powling
Jacket Design Assistant Rosie Levine
Pre-production Producer Sarah Isle
Producer Jen Lockwood
Art Directors Peter Luff, Jane Bull
Publisher Mary Ling
Special Sales Creative Project Manager Alison Donovan

DK India
Editors Vibha Malhotra, Arani Sinha
Art Editors Ranjita Bhattacharji, Devan Das
DTP Manager Sunil Sharma
DTP Designers Sourabh Challariya, Arjinder Singh

Tall Tree Ltd
Editor Emma Marriott
Designer Ben Ruocco

Written by Anya Hayes

First published in Great Britain in 2013
This paperback edition published in 2014 by
Dorling Kindersley Limited, 80 Strand, London WC2R 0RL

A Penguin Random House Comapny

2 4 6 8 10 9 7 5 3 1
001–187846–Jun/2014

A CIP catalogue record for this book is available from the British Library.

ISBN 978-1-4093-7214-1

Printed and bound by Leo Paper Products Ltd, China

Discover more at
www.dk.com

Contents

PUBLISHER'S NOTE
Neither the publisher nor the author is engaged in rendering professional advice or services to the individual reader. The ideas, procedures, and suggestions contained in this book are not intended as a substitute for consulting with your physician. All matters regarding your health require medical supervision. Neither the author nor the publisher shall be liable or responsible for any loss or damage allegedly arising from any information or suggestion in this book.

Build Your Course

This book is divided into three sections: Start Simple, Build On It, and Take It Further. As you progress through the book the positions gradually become more challenging and you will increase your physical ability, while also learning how to plan and assess your sessions.

Getting Started

In order to get the most from Pilates it is important to understand the ideas that underpin it. The introduction to this book guides you through the key principles of Pilates, from centring to breathing, and explains its benefits, which range from flexibility and alignment to toning and shaping. As well as delving a little deeper into the science of posture and breathing, it will show you the equipment you'll need.

1 In every section, illustrated step-by-step text guides you carefully through the exercises. The text explains in detail exactly how you need to position yourself.

Careful! To guide you and give further useful advice, key information about each step is flagged up, helping you to avoid common mistakes.

Take care and Make it easier

It can be easy to think that you are performing an exercise correctly when in fact you're not. Some movements could strain your body if done incorrectly, so it's crucial not to make mistakes. The useful "Take care" boxes will teach you how to check and correct your posture, so you don't make common mistakes. Some boxes have illustrations so that you can clearly see how a movement should not be performed. If you are struggling with a difficult exercise, "Make it easier" boxes advise you how to modify the move so it's less of a strain.

Planning and Assessing

It's important to plan your sessions so that you can set yourself goals and keep track of how hard you're working. It is also crucial to take a step back now and again to assess your progress and check that you aren't making any mistakes. At the beginning and end of each section are pages that will help you to create plans to reach specific goals, such as improving your centring or alignment, and pages that will help you to assess your progress (see the two examples below). They also answer common questions that you might have and offer helpful advice and guidance so you can achieve your goals.

Week 1: Focus on Alignment

Baseline: take photos of yourself standing – front, side, and back – and draw plumb lines on the images, as on pp.20–21.

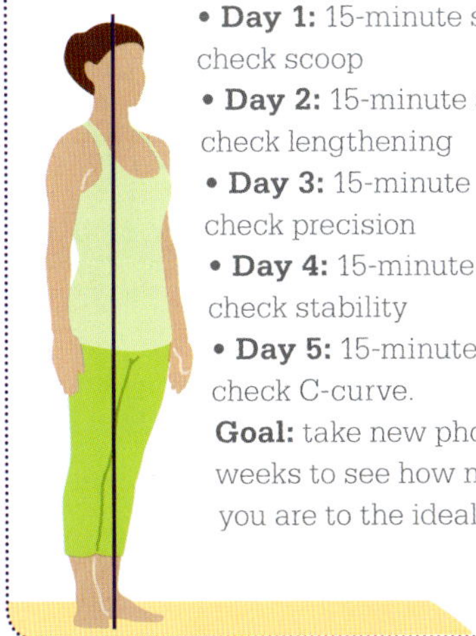

- **Day 1:** 15-minute sequence, check scoop
- **Day 2:** 15-minute sequence, check lengthening
- **Day 3:** 15-minute sequence, check precision
- **Day 4:** 15-minute sequence, check stability
- **Day 5:** 15-minute sequence, check C-curve.

Goal: take new photos after six weeks to see how much closer you are to the ideal alignment.

Goal: Centring

Centring (see p.40)

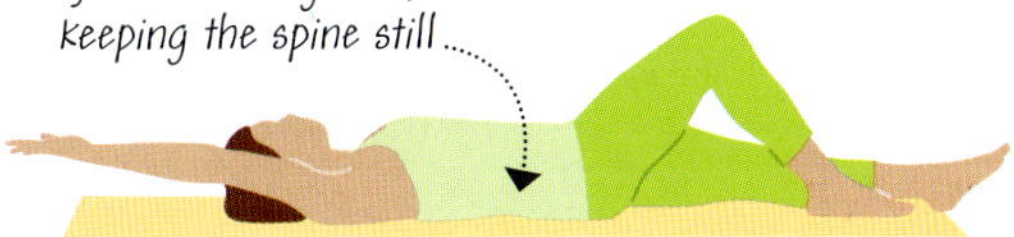

Goal: Strength

Wall: Chair (see p.45), Hundred Preparation (see pp.54–55), Roll Up (see pp.58–59)

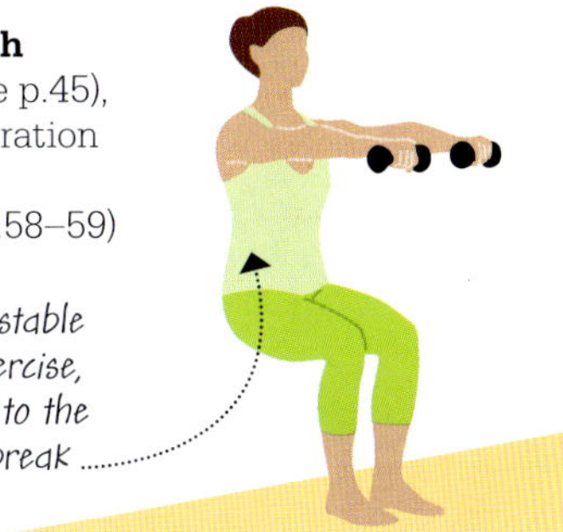

Sequences

Once you've mastered the positions, the next step is to put them together and practise them as a sequence. At the end of each section is a selection of timed sequences for you to follow: choose from 15 , 30, and 45 minutes. The sequences give the names of the movements and their page references, so that you can flick back to check that you are doing them correctly.

1 **Pilates Stance** p.35

2 **Wall: Roll Down** pp.42–43

3 **Wall: Stand** p.44

The 6 Principles of Pilates

Joe Pilates based his body conditioning system on six principles. Hold them in mind every time you work out and your practice will be infinitely more effective, becoming second nature over time. As Pilates said, these principles combine "to give you suppleness, natural grace and skill".

1. Control

This is the most important principle from which all other Pilates principles derive. Joe Pilates's original name for his exercise system was Contrology. According to his philosophy, a few movements performed correctly – with complete muscular and mental control and purposeful, precise movement – were more effective than many repetitions performed sloppily. This applies to ALL movement, be it slow, swift, or dynamic. Control enables you to become more aware of where your body is in space and to work targeted muscles effectively.

Key points

- **Consider the execution** of every part of the movement. Control everything: alignment, breathing, pace, coordination...
- **Be certain about the exercise.** Memorize the breath pattern and movement so you can begin to control the entire exercise effectively. There should be no uncertainty in your movement.
- **Control the movement**: beginning, middle, and end. Always move with fluidity, strength, and precision. Never simply slump onto the mat at the end of a repetition.

How Joe developed Pilates: Joseph Pilates studied anatomy and trained as a body builder, gymnast, and boxer. He developed his exercise regime after the First World War in New York, where it was quickly taken up by ballet dancers as well as the city's elite. "Pilates Elders", who had trained directly with him, spread his work throughout the world. Some taught "classical" Pilates, exactly as he had taught them. Others developed the exercises in their own ways. Pilates continues to evolve today.

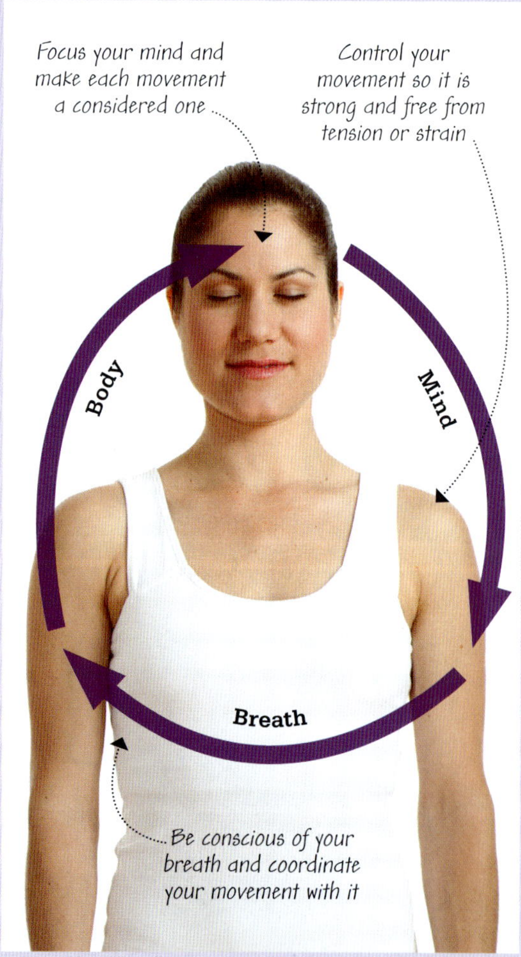

2. Concentration

Pilates requires deep focus on your body – as Joe Pilates said, "complete coordination of body, mind and spirit". Your success in Pilates will hinge on your ability to concentrate on the precise detail of every movement, and so develop body awareness and control.

Be strict with yourself: never let your mind wander or run on autopilot and perform mindless repetitions while you're working out. Always concentrate on the task in hand and your exercise will be much more effective and you will see results faster. This mental connection with your body while you move allows you to release tension and encourages a deep sense of relaxation, by emptying your mind of all other thoughts or worries.

Key points

- **Don't try to focus on the whole body** at once. Think about which muscles you're working, and focus on one part of your body or on your breathing. With practice, you'll be able to concentrate effectively on your whole body with ease.
- **Run through a checklist in your mind** as you work out. Think about lengthening parts of your body, how you breathe, if you're engaging your powerhouse. Being your own teacher reaps great rewards.
- **Concentrate and correct yourself** as you move. Focus on perfecting the movement: notice if your alignment is off, if you have lost abdominal engagement, or if your neck is tense.

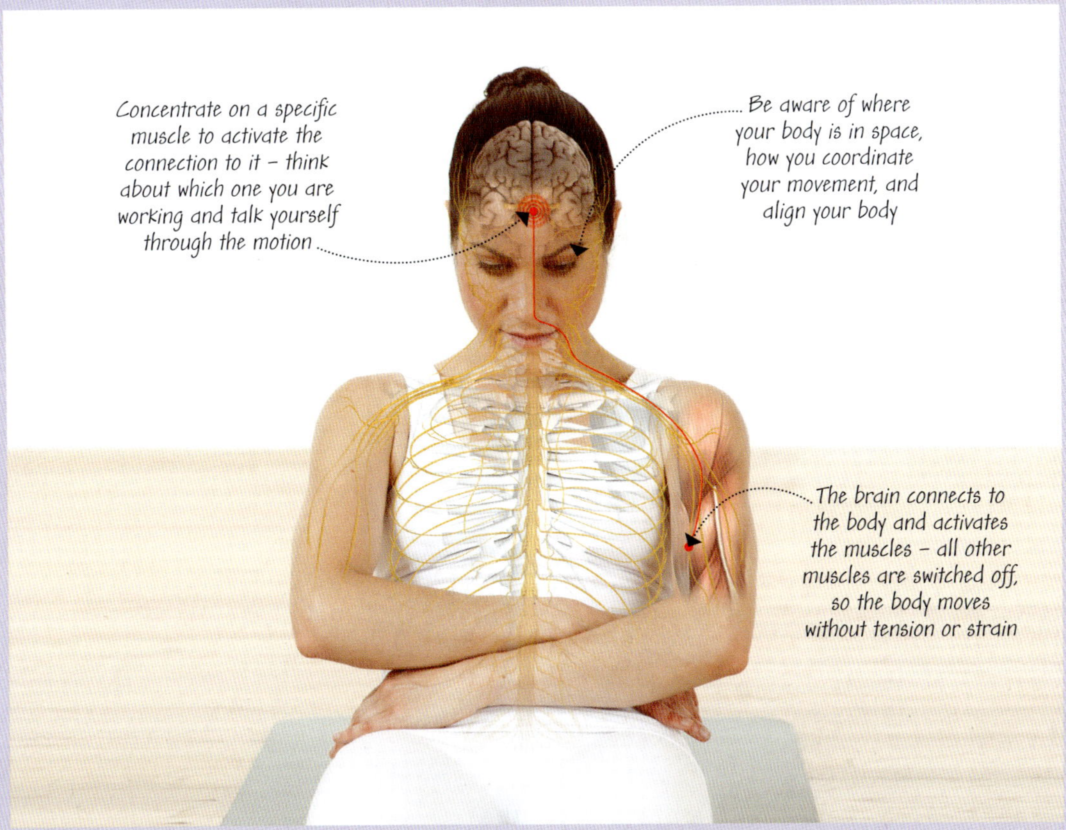

3. Centring

Joe Pilates' taught that energy in movement "flows from a strong centre". He noticed that drawing in the belly "navel to spine", tightening the muscles like a corset around his waist, supported his spine and made it strong. He called this the "powerhouse" or "girdle of strength". Physically, the "centre" is your core muscles: the pelvic floor and deep, lower abdominals. The powerhouse – upper abdominals, buttocks, and inner-thigh muscles – provides strength for your movement. Centring also involves a mindful connection to your body as you move. Be aware of your centre to begin and end each movement, so you never lose the connection.

Key points

- **Lift up your pelvic floor** and draw in the belly, to tighten the powerhouse and create strength. Think "pull in and up".
- **Always pause briefly at the end** of a move, to ensure your concentration and centre connection are still strong.
- **Think of your centre as a dimmer switch**: it is always on, but at different brightnesses. Turn it to full brightness, or full engagement, for very hard work or to low engagement for basic exercises.

4. Precision

Precise, mindful execution of the movement and perfect alignment is key to effective Pilates. Moving with precision works the muscles correctly without strain or tension. Correctly aligning your body balances your muscles. Practise giving every aspect of your exercise equal attention, to make each movement more precise and gain more from your workout. Precision also applies to the number of repetitions, your timing and pace: bring balance and determination to every aspect of each movement. Memorize the actions and breath patterns of an exercise beforehand, then work on its precise execution. Practice to gain control and skill.

Key points

- **No part of the exercise** should be an afterthought.
- **Imagine your body as an orchestra:** not all instruments take centre stage throughout, but all are key to the whole performance. Every part of your body is involved – be aware of what each does throughout.
- **Give equal weight in your mind** to each element of the movement and perform it with care.

5. Breath

Oxygen is vital for correct working of muscles; focusing on the breath ensures they are fully oxygenated during a movement. We breathe in through the nose and out through the mouth, relaxing the jaw and face. Pilates uses "lateral breathing": it channels wide into the body's back and sides so the ribcage expands at the sides as you breathe in, rather than the belly rising forwards. Your connection to your centre, the abdominals, can then stay strong as you breathe and move. Synchronizing the breath to movement is fundamental in Pilates. We often exhale on the effortful movement to help engage the deep core muscles effectively.

Key points

- **Often in daily life we breathe shallowly** into our chests. In Pilates, lateral breathing encourages a deeper inhalation, effectively charging your body with fresh oxygen and benefiting your skin, muscles, and blood.
- **Time your breath to the movement.** At first, it seems odd, but with practice it becomes second nature.
- **You should hear your out breath,** like a sigh through soft lips. Don't forget to breathe! If you hold your breath during a movement, you will tense up.

6. Flowing movements

When practising Pilates, you should have a silent pulse in your mind, like a metronome or the pulsing of your heart. Perform all exercises synchronized with this pulse and the breath, aiming for continuous, fluid movement. Each exercise is created to flow seamlessly into the next in sequence, with no wasted movement in transition. This ensures a full-body workout that keeps up the heart rate and builds stamina and endurance.

Key points

- **Even in a short workout**, keep your focus and choreograph the sequence of exercises to flow without resting.
- **Pilates appears balletic, strong**, effortless, and not laboured, if performed correctly. Aim for the grace and fluidity of a dancer.

The 6 Key Benefits of Pilates

Pilates exercises combine strengthening with relaxation; they lighten the load on your spine and joints by correcting muscular imbalances due to bad posture or misuse of muscles and alleviate tension. You'll rediscover your body's natural movement patterns and experience six key benefits.

1. Alignment

Proper alignment balances your skeleton so your muscles are held at their ideal length, without tension. If your body is constantly held out of good alignment, it places a great strain on your muscles, ligaments, and joints, which will reduce your body's ability to react to the force of gravity, resulting in aches and pains and inhibited movement. Pilates gives you an opportunity to learn to correct your misalignments and allow your muscles to work as efficiently as they should.

As you exercise, always strive to correct your alignment because it will directly impact on the effectiveness of your workout. Use a mirror where possible to check your alignment and develop your ability to observe how your body moves. Check your feet are in line with your knees and hips, your shoulders are level, and your waist long. For floor exercises, use the mat as a guide. Work in the centre and keep the distances between the sides of the mat and your body equal during the workout.

Key benefits

- **The impact of gravity on your spine** and joints will be reduced every day, whether you are moving or at rest.
- **The risk of strain or injury is lessened** with good alignment, particularly with more challenging and dynamic exercises.
- **Improvements in your posture,** how you carry yourself, and how you move every day result from awareness of body alignment.

2. Strength

Pilates is a wonderful body-conditioning programme because you don't need any equipment in order to strengthen your body. You can simply use your own body weight to create resistance for your muscles and to tone up. Which truly does mean that your workout will be only as effective as the effort you put in to the exercises. Strength begins with a determination to achieve the best. Over time, you will see your muscles gaining tone and looking sculpted, but you'll also feel much stronger and more energized.

Pilates strengthens the whole body, targeting each muscle group evenly with a mixture of dynamic and static strength training. No body part is neglected. You also work on all planes of movement – sitting, lying, standing. This means that the muscles are worked from many different directions, producing a uniform and very deep strength and tone, even without using heavy weights.

Key benefits

- **You are less likely to suffer** from muscular and joint aches and pains, or to injure yourself, because your balance and the way you carry yourself will improve.
- **You rev up your metabolism** by building muscle, so that even when not exercising your stronger body burns more calories.
- **Strength leads to greater health:** by committing to a Pilates way of life, you will lower your blood pressure and reduce your cholesterol levels.
- **Pilates builds strength from the inside out,** from your deep core muscles, so that they support your body effectively in movement, and outwards to the limbs.
- **Reduced tension and strain in the body** results from a strong core, which will also allow your muscles to be free to work with an intensity that will create great results.

3. Flexibility

We all want to achieve a strong body, but there must be a balance between strength and flexibility, and Pilates is the perfect exercise regime to achieve this. Tight muscles hinder your mobility and can lead to tension, aches, and pain. Flexibility is essential for your overall fitness and vitality. It ensures a greater range of movement in your joints, and will in turn mean your joints remain healthy and fare better against normal wear and tear as they age.

Pilates makes most use of dynamic, rather than static, stretching: this involves taking your body into and out of a stretch repeatedly, in a choreographed movement. It warms up the muscles so that they respond more effectively. As you progress through the exercises in this book, you should find your range of movement increasing and your flexibility improving.

Key benefits

- **Your muscles are free from tension,** and your movement is unrestricted, when you achieve good flexibility.
- **Your posture will improve,** because you will be able to hold your muscles correctly.
- **Better blood circulation** results from improved flexibility, because it helps the muscles to align more effectively. Improved circulation also gives you a boost of energy.
- **Joints stay healthy as you age:** they resist wear and tear better if they are flexible and move freely.

4. Shape and tone

For a lot of us, our muscle tone while at rest may be quite weak. Muscles respond quickly to regular exercise, and after a few weeks of Pilates you should notice visible muscle tone and see your body begin to evolve. The Pilates in this book uses only your body weight and the occasional prop as resistance for shaping your muscles, but it trains every part of your body evenly – front, back, and sides.

For example, during an abdominal exercise, don't think only about engaging your centre or belly, but be aware of lengthening your limbs, lifting your buttocks, and connecting your shoulders. If you also combine exercise with proper diet to reduce body fat, you'll notice your muscle tone become even more defined.

Key benefits

- **Develop more muscle definition** through Pilates exercise – sculpt your waist and shoulders and tone your abdominals, arms, thighs, and your buttocks.
- **Change your body shape** completely with regular practice of Pilates. With work, you should see a beautifully toned and lengthened body emerge.

5. Endurance

Pilates builds endurance within individual exercises and also within workouts. Focus on improving your concentration to build strength for both – endurance comes first from mental strength and therefore requires determination and persistence. Visualize your success and becoming stronger, and stay strong through challenging exercises.

You should practise Pilates sequences without breaks, like a choreographed piece of movement. Initially, you may need to take breaks to perform a linked sequence of exercises. Your muscles will begin to tire after several repetitions, but you need to stay focused and to complete the set. Over time, work towards completing a sequence without pausing.

Key benefits

- **Pilates builds stamina,** not only physical, but mental.
- **Immense strength and tone** in the body is developed in Pilates by using your own body weight.
- **Improved concentration** results from focusing on completing each repetition, exercise, and sequence.

6. Stress Relief

Stress is one of the biggest negative factors of modern life, affecting your physical and mental wellbeing just as much as disease does. Frequent exercise is one of the best remedies for stress and has many benefits. Pilates focuses on breathing – a deep, mindful pattern of breathing that instantly enhances feelings of calm and release in the body and mind. We also work constantly on posture: a poised and lifted body, free from tension and pain, creates a calm mind.

Release the tension...

Lying on your mat: before your workout, give in to gravity and consciously release the muscles of the entire body into the floor. Soften the jaw, neck, and shoulders. Feel your worries sink into the mat and leave them there.

The Child's Pose is useful for releasing tension in the back after a challenging exercise. From lying on your front, push your bottom back onto the heels; keep a rounded back and engaged centre. Open the knees slightly wider than the hips, to allow the upper body to sink towards the floor. Extend the arms along the mat in front of the head. Inhale to stretch and release the lower back muscles; engage the centre more as you exhale.

Key benefits

- **A sense of calm and wellbeing** is encouraged by the relaxation of tense muscles during Pilates.
- **Pilates releases endorphins**, which naturally cause the body and mind to feel more relaxed and positive.
- **Your sleep will improve** with regular Pilates, which will greatly reduce any fatigue and stress.
- **You will feel energized and invigorated,** because Pilates forces you to focus on the present moment and the movement you are performing, to the exclusion of your everyday preoccupations and stresses.

The Science of **Anatomy**

Muscles create movement or stability in the skeleton, holding the bones in correct alignment. Pilates is a unique system that trains the body evenly, restoring balance to muscles and freeing them to perform efficiently. This encourages fluidity of movement and makes you less prone to injury.

Poor posture or overuse makes muscles tight and short, or weak and long. Pilates forces you to focus on isolating certain body parts and individual or groups of muscles, so you can't use the wrong ones. Understanding more about the musculo-skeletal system will enable you to have greater awareness of how to control your body in movement.

Imagine your body as an orchestra: like instruments, your muscles should be correctly placed, tuned, and in harmony with each other, and working at the right tempo and volume, with all the bones in the proper placement. Then, you will create the correct movement and work the intended muscles – and soon see them become toned and defined.

In Pilates, muscles work together to create balance, strength, and stamina. You use your own body weight – and props such as hand weights – to create a sculpted and toned body.

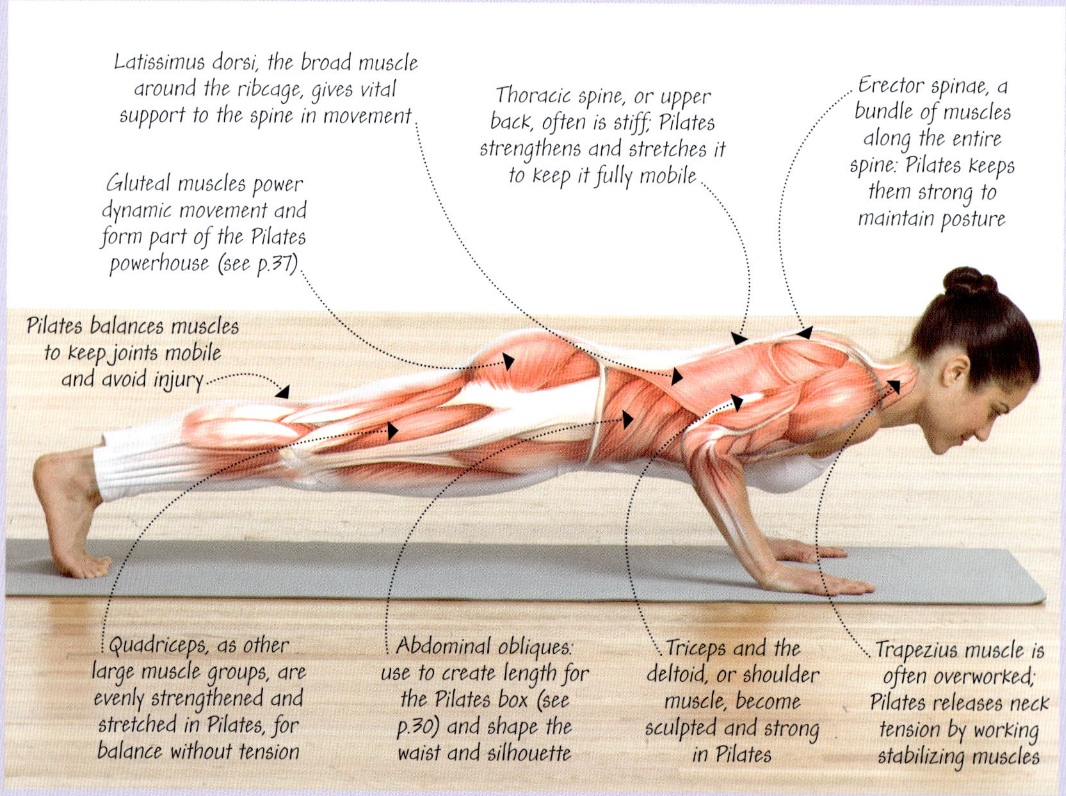

There are several layers of abdominal muscles and Pilates strengthens each layer. The deepest muscles closest to the spine, such as the crucial, core muscles *transversus abdominis*, work constantly. More superficial muscles near the skin, such as the obliques and the *rectus abdominis*, tone with movement.

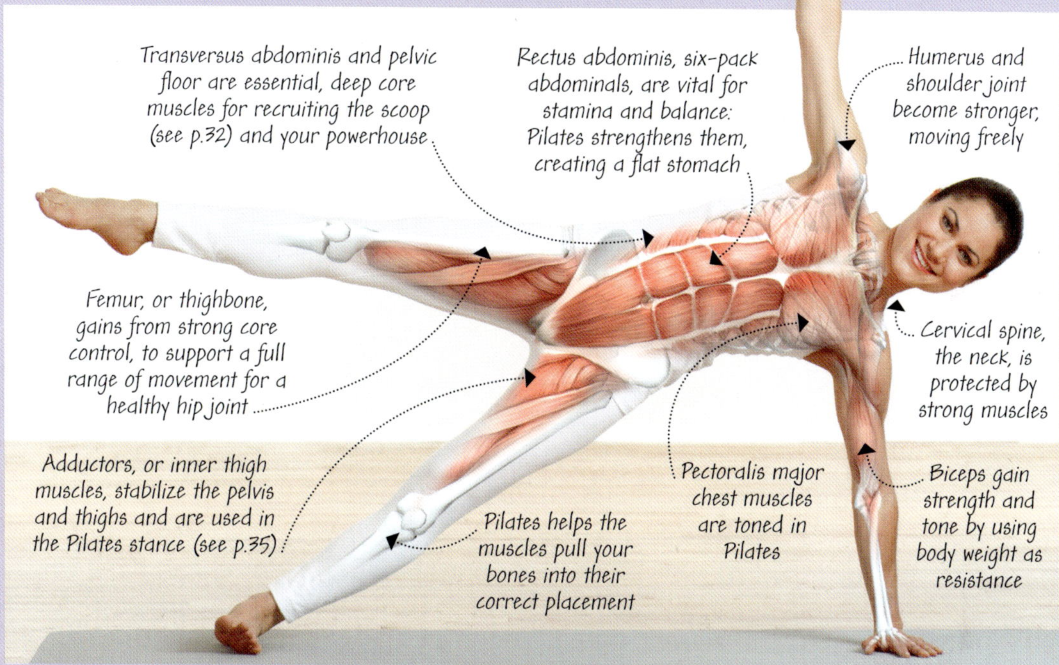

The core muscles – the *transversus abdominis* and pelvic floor – are strengthened in Pilates to provide stability for the pelvis and spine, so every muscle is free to move efficiently without overworking.

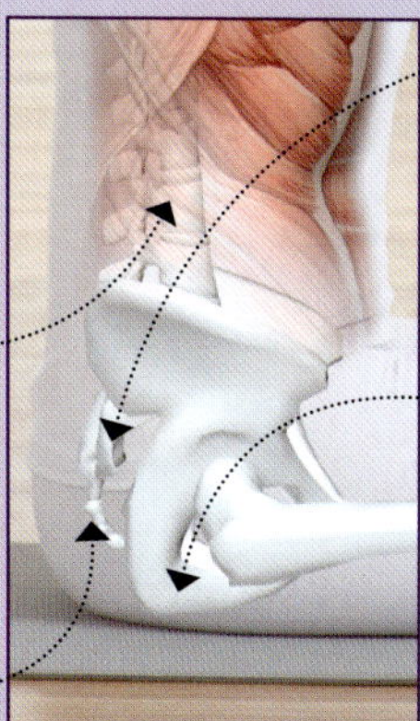

Powerhouse muscles

Use the muscles in your Pilates powerhouse to maintain strength and control in dynamic movements.

- Lift the pelvic floor first (hammock of muscles in the pelvis); glide the sitting bones together to engage the muscles, then feel them rising as if moving up floors in a lift.
- Pull in the lower belly towards the spine to increase engagement and create the "scoop" (see p.32).
- Squeeze your buttocks and inner thighs to start limb movements from a strong, stable core.

The Science of **Alignment**

Pilates trains you to use the deep core muscles of the powerhouse - the abdominals, back, and pelvic floor - to support your posture and bring your skeleton into alignment, so you can move correctly and efficiently.

If the body is constantly held out of good alignment, it puts a great strain on the muscles and joints, compresses the organs, and limits your capacity for deep breathing. This will hinder your body's ability to react against the constant pull of gravity and result in pain and restricted mobility.

Rather than holding your posture with the wrong muscles (such as those around the neck and shoulders, or buttocks) and creating tension where there shouldn't be any, Pilates teaches you how to use your core so your muscles are balanced. It helps you to correct your misalignments and imbalances and achieve the optimal placing of your muscles.

This will allow the shoulders to relax, the neck and head to move freely, and will relieve stress on the lower body. You know good posture when you see it – and we are all inspired by the confidence and strength it radiates.

Side view of ideal alignment: If a plumb line were dropped through the centre of the body, it would fall through the middle of the ear and the shoulder, just behind the hip joint, and just in front of the ankle joint. Try to imagine this plumb line with your own posture, every day.

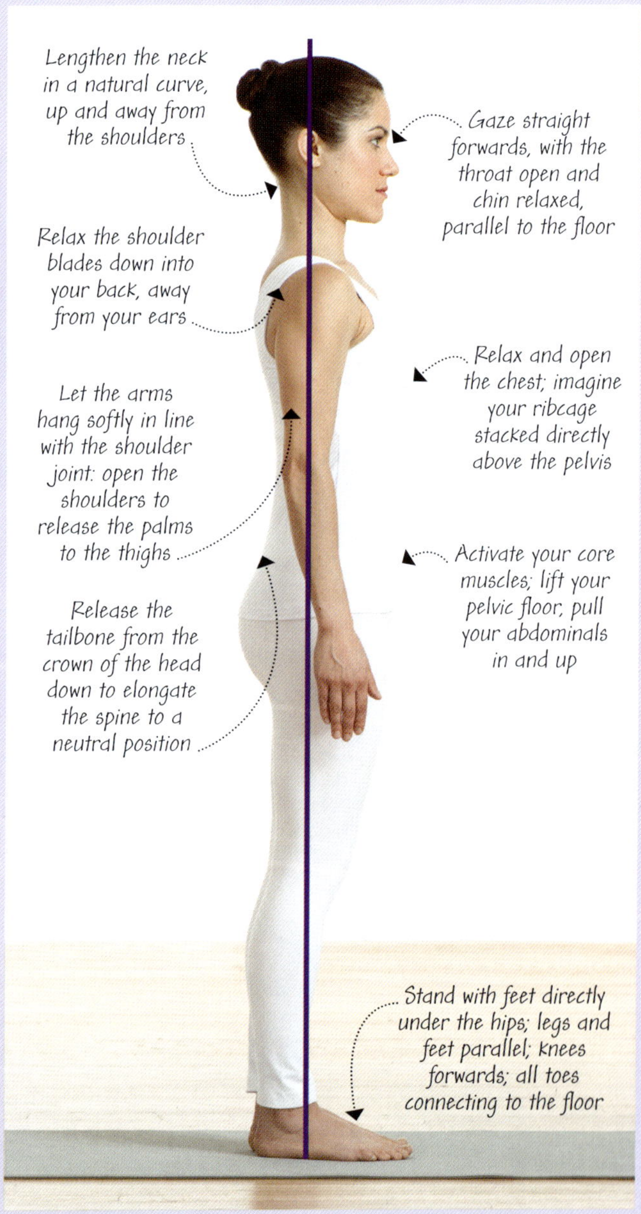

Front view of alignment: Imagine you have a space between each vertebra of your spine. Feel these spaces lengthening and the bones lifting up, away from each other, as you grow taller.

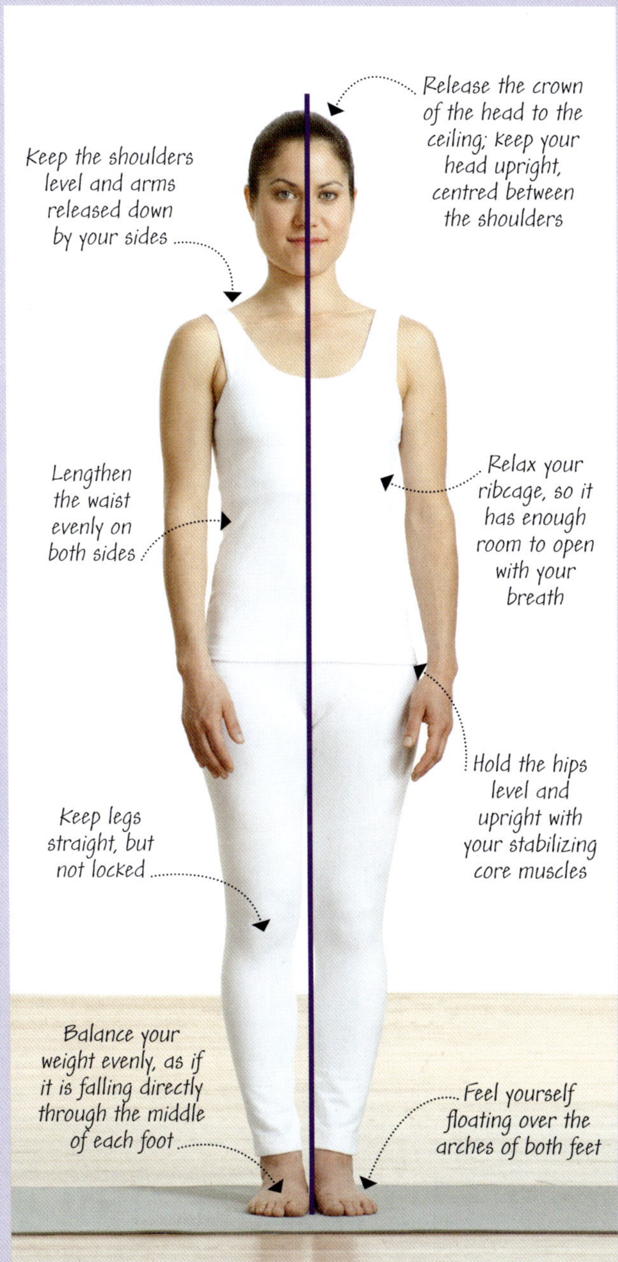

Science in practice

Good alignment is important to the effectiveness of Pilates exercises, so you work the correct muscles and relax parts that shouldn't be working. Proper alignment also lessens the risk of strain or injury.

- Constantly check your alignment: ensure your feet are in line with the hips, your pelvis is square, and your neck is relaxed and long.
- Use a mirror and mat as a guide for each workout. Work in the centre of the mat, keeping the distances between the mat edges and both sides of your body equal as you proceed through the workout.
- Be aware of alignment to improve how you move on a daily basis.

What not to do

The Science of **Breathing**

Joe Pilates said, "Above all, learn to breathe correctly." Deep breathing coordinated with movement forms the foundation of all of his exercises. Carry this breathing skill into your daily life and you'll feel energized and calmed, your blood pressure will reduce, and your circulation will improve.

The benefits of efficient, deep breathing, or lateral breathing, cannot be underestimated, yet in daily life so often we forget to breathe fully. Joe Pilates saw breathing as a way of cleansing the lungs – he wanted us to "wring the air out of the lungs as water out of a wet cloth". He felt that the exhalation was the most important part of the breath, because a full and long exhalation naturally encourages a deep and wide inhalation, which oxygenates and nourishes the blood and muscles.

Coordinating the breath to the movement is a skill that requires practice and it is what confuses most people when they first begin Pilates. Lateral breathing is an integral part of the Pilates workout: drawing in long, deep breaths wide into the sides of the ribcage, followed by a long, full exhalation to deflate the lungs entirely. The exhalation helps to engage the deep abdominal muscles. You can practise lateral breathing while standing up (see opposite) or lying on the mat.

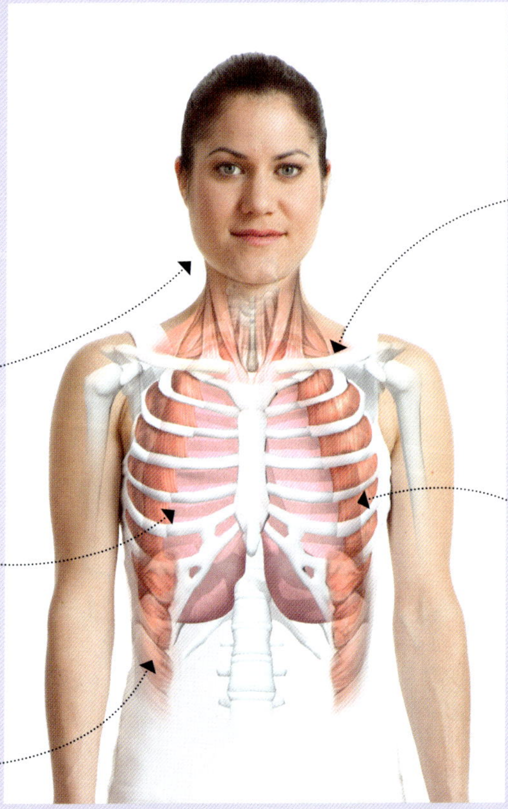

Correct lateral breathing Inhaling wide into the ribcage exercises the muscles around the ribcage as the lungs expand on the in breath.

Breathing in Inhale through the nose, channelling the air fully into the back of the body. Under your hands feel the ribcage expanding sideways with the breath. Soften the shoulders away from the ears.

Breathing out Sigh the breath out through the mouth; relax the jaw. Think of the lungs as bellows, squeezing the air out as the waist muscles wrap around and close the ribs. Feel the ribcage narrow.

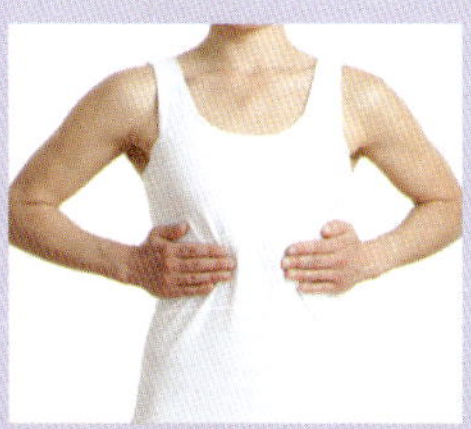

Science in Practice

The exhalation helps to deeply engage the abdominal muscles.

- Perform movements that need the most powerhouse engagement and effort, such as curling the upper body off the mat, on the out breath.
- Don't let the belly expand with the breath: as you breathe in the ribcage expands, then the abdominals contract to expel the out breath.

The Pilates breathing pattern is used to help with the final movement in the Saw (see pp.162–163).

The Hundred (see pp.144–145) is the quintessential breathing exercise. You need to coordinate your breath with your movement and breathe efficiently, without tension, as you use the core abdominals.

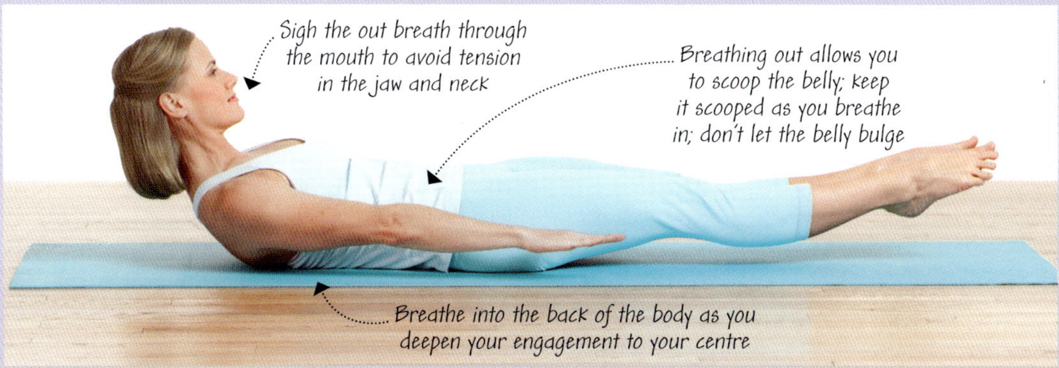

Essential **Equipment**

For Pilates, all you really need is yourself, but this equipment will help you to get the most out of your practice. It is all available online or from sports outlets. Wear comfortable, form-fitting clothes without stitching, buttons, or seams that might cause discomfort when you lie on them. There's no need for shoes: you need to connect your feet into the floor. If you can, work out in front of a mirror, so you can check your alignment.

Magic circle
These are not usually expensive and greatly enhance your workout.

Stretchy band
These are available in various resistances, or colours: choose a medium-strength band.

Pilates mat
In Pilates, you need to cushion the spine, so this is thicker than a yoga mat. You could use a thick towel or a blanket, but make sure your spine is comfortable in movement.

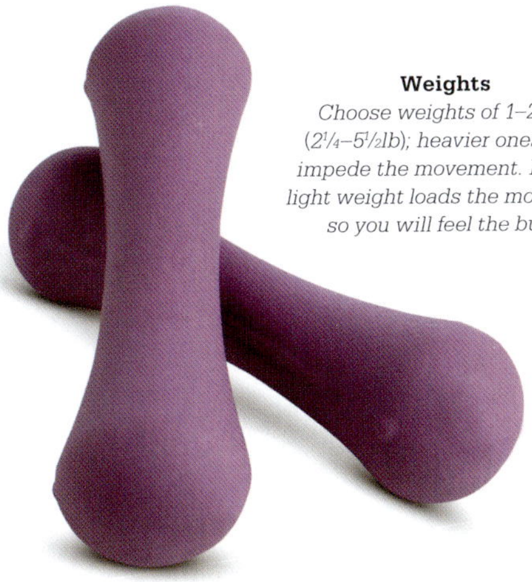

Weights

Choose weights of 1–2.5kg (2¼–5½lb); heavier ones may impede the movement. Even a light weight loads the movement so you will feel the burn.

Towel

Have a towel to hand – the dynamic exercises get the blood pumping and work up a sweat!

Small cushion

You may use this under your head when lying on the mat. Always remove it for exercises such as pelvic curls (see p.39) or roll overs (see pp.146–147), where you lift your lower spine, to avoid compressing the neck.

Water bottle

It's important to stay hydrated; if you feel dizzy or light-headed, stop at once.

1

Start Simple

Now that you understand the fundamental principles behind Pilates, you are ready to start putting theory into practice. In this first section, you will be guided through some key techniques and exercises, so that you can create a solid foundation of skills and movements and start developing an awareness of your body's weaknesses and strengths. By the end of this chapter, you will be able to put together what you've learned into an exercise sequence.

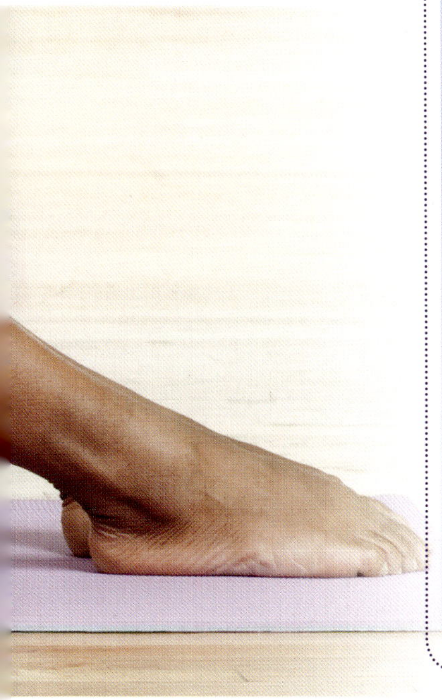

Plan Your Programme

Joe Pilates said "In 10 sessions you will feel the difference, in 20 you will see the difference, and in 30 you will have a whole new body." Congratulations on committing to Pilates – if you put in the effort, you will soon begin to feel the benefits.

Planning your course

Pilates is a total-body conditioning programme; it does not strain the muscles or joints, so the body doesn't need a rest. You can practise every day. (If you have injuries or spinal issues, check with your doctor first.) Take time to understand the key techniques, principles, and exercises. Work through all the warm-up exercises in Key Techniques (see pp.30–39) for your first session. The first week, follow a 15-minute Key Technique sequence each day – try to perfect each technique and become familiar with the muscular engagement. Then begin the Start Simple programme. Aim to apply the six Pilates principles every time you practise.

Start Simple Exercise Programme

Use this programme to set yourself goals and assess your progress over the next six weeks. (Sequence summaries are on pp.80–85). Each week, follow the sequences exactly and focus on one area. As the weeks pass, more will be added until, by the end of the course, you should feel comfortable concentrating on multiple aspects of your movement. Then you could substitute other exercises with the same level of proficiency, as long as they train the same body area, for a balanced workout. Pilates is all about detail. Be your own coach: check every movement. If you find it easy, you may not be performing it attentively.

Week 1: Focus on Alignment

Baseline: take photos of yourself standing – front, side and back – and draw plumb lines on the images, as on pp.20–21.

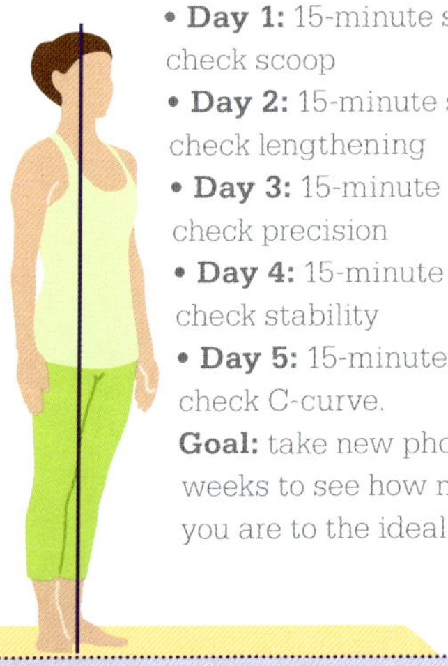

- **Day 1:** 15-minute sequence, check scoop
- **Day 2:** 15-minute sequence, check lengthening
- **Day 3:** 15-minute sequence, check precision
- **Day 4:** 15-minute sequence, check stability
- **Day 5:** 15-minute sequence, check C-curve.

Goal: take new photos after six weeks to see how much closer you are to the ideal alignment.

Week 2: Focus on Control

Baseline: perform the Roll Back (see pp.56–57). Are you shaking, tensing, or misaligned, or moving jerkily? Is your Pilates box square?

- **Day 1**: 15-minute sequence, check centring, alignment
- **Day 2**: 30-minute sequence, check concentration, precision
- **Day 3:** 15-minute sequence, check precision, breathing
- **Day 4:** 30-minute sequence, check flowing movement, stability
- **Day 5:** 15-minute sequence, check lengthening, breathing.

Goal: do the exercise with control, precision and fluidity, remembering to breathe, scoop, and lengthen.

Week 3: Focus on Centring

Baseline: perform the Centring exercise (see p.40). Is the spine supported and strong as you move? Is the back arched?

- **Day 1:** 15-minute sequence, check Pilates box, alignment, flowing movement
- **Day 2:** 30-minute sequence, check stability, precision, lengthening
- **Day 3:** 45-minute sequence, check precision, control, breathing
- **Day 4:** 30-minute sequence, check control, alignment
- **Day 5:** 15-minute sequence, check alignment, scoop.

Goal: Performing the exercise with no spinal movement as you lengthen the limbs away, smoothly and controlled.

Week 4: Focus on Flexibility

Baseline: perform Wall: Roll Down (see pp.42–43). Does your spine feel mobile and fluid or stiff and inflexible?

- **Day 1:** 15-minute sequence, check precision, control, alignment
- **Day 2:** 30-minute sequence, check breathing, scoop, stability
- **Day 3:** 45-minute sequence, check scoop, powerhouse, coordination.
- **Day 4:** 30-minute sequence, check control, concentration
- **Day 5:** 15-minute sequence, check alignment, flowing movement.

Goal: Moving fluidly, bone by bone, and achieving even sequential movement through each part of the spine.

Week 5: Focus on Strength

Baseline: perform Wall: Chair (see p.45), Hundred Preparation (see pp.54–55), and Roll Up, pp.58–59) without a break. On a scale of 1–10, how hard is each exercise and sequence?

- **Day 1:** 15-minute sequence, check centring, control, coordination
- **Day 2:** 45-minute sequence, check scoop, alignment, concentration
- **Day 3:** 15-minute sequence, check flowing movement, alignment, coordination
- **Day 4:** 30-minute sequence, check control, precision, powerhouse
- **Day 5:** 45-minute sequence, check flowing movement, breathing.

Goal: Performing the sequence should feel easier.

Week 6: Focus on Flowing Movement

Baseline: perform Single Leg Stretch 1 (see p.64). Are you moving fluidly or jerkily? Can you link both leg movements smoothly?

- **Day 1:** 30-minute sequence, check centring, breathing, coordination
- **Day 2:** 45-minute sequence, check stability, control, Pilates box
- **Day 3:** 15-minute sequence, check alignment, precision, coordination
- **Day 4:** 30-minute sequence, check precision, centring, breathing
- **Day 5:** 45-minute sequence, check control, powerhouse, concentration.

Goal: Do the exercise swiftly, changing from side to side without wobbling or stopping.

There is a lot to take on board when you start Pilates, but as you gain confidence and skill, your practice will improve. Pilates will lift your spirits and give you a new body. Your breathing, stamina, and strength will improve; you'll move more gracefully and see muscle definition and a sculpted shape emerging. Enjoy the next six weeks!

Key Techniques to Practise

In Pilates there are a few fundamental positions you need to master to ensure your workout is safe and effective. Practise these positions until you feel them confidently and correctly in your body, and revisit them regularly as you advance through the levels.

The Pilates box

This box is your reference for checking your alignment, making sure your muscles are balanced, and reminding you to work symmetrically and safely. Check that your box remains square while you move. Be aware of whether you're twisted or shortening on one side. Train yourself to notice differences in length on either side of your body.

Neutral spine

Arching the back

Tucking under

The neutral spine

Neutral spine encourages length in the spine, in its natural curve. In neutral, muscles are switched off, perfectly balanced, and your body primed for movement. As you lie flat on the floor, roll through the pelvis, tilting forwards and back. Gradually decrease the movement and come to a point where you're neither arched nor tucking. This is neutral.

Bad scoop

Good scoop

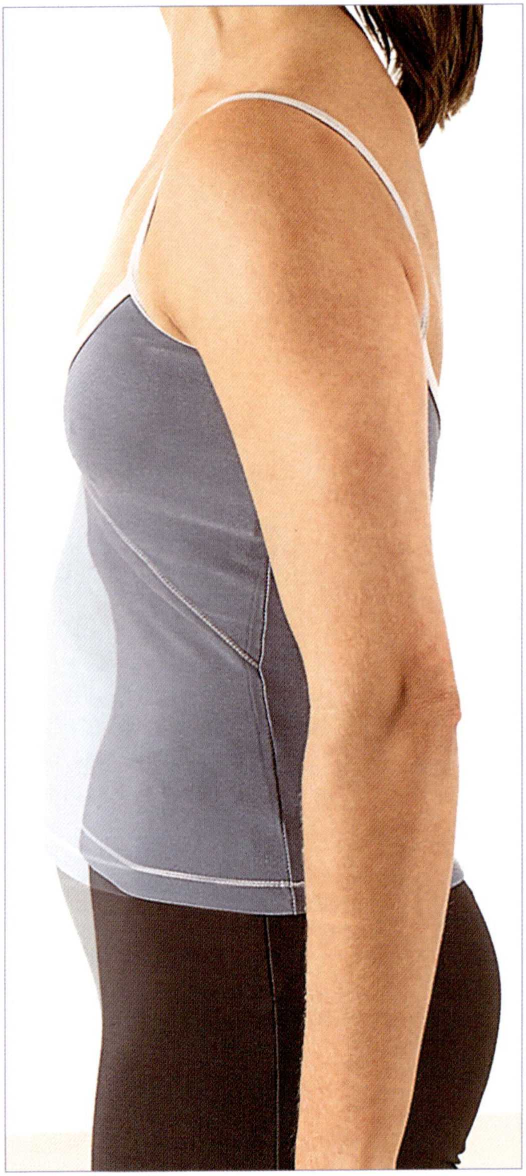

Standing scoop

The scoop

The scoop should look and feel as if you're hollowing your abdominals up and in. The abdominals should move deep towards the spine, pinning your navel like a mattress button, without affecting the natural curve of your spine. It should feel as if you're pulling in a corset, tightly drawing the waist in and up, and engaging the lower abdominals.

Lengthening

In Pilates we continually aim to lengthen our body using our muscles: to elongate the waist by lifting the ribs away from the hips and create space between each vertebra of the spine, growing taller and longer throughout the movement. You will often see directions to "lift", "lengthen", and "reach". Every movement is consciously sustaining a long spine and limbs, so you are aware of your posture and every part of your body, even if it's not moving. After a good Pilates session you should feel taller, and you may literally be!

Tip The core, also called the "centre", refers to a layer of muscles that encircle the spine and pelvis. They are stabilizing muscles as they create strength and support the spine, but they do not control the dynamic movement of the spine or limbs. The core, along with mobilizing muscles, forms the powerhouse (see p.37). Also see Science of Anatomy on p.18.

Stabilizing

In Pilates we need to keep the torso stable as we move. This means that no unwanted movement should occur in the body while we move our limbs. To do this, we need to engage our core muscles: the pelvic floor, deep abdominals, and spinal muscles. This supports and stabilizes the spine, and enables the limbs to move freely without tension.

Warm-up Exercises

Before each Pilates workout you must warm up your body. Take a few minutes to practise one, or all, of these exercises to mobilize the spine, focus on your breathing, and relax your muscles in preparation for movement. The seated C-curve (see p.36) and Pilates stance (see opposite) are positions that you need to create in many exercises shown in this book. Learn to engage your powerhouse (see p.37) correctly to move with energy, stability, strength, and control. Remember to practise your key techniques as you perform these exercises.

The table top

This is an exercise in concentration and alignment, requiring strength and balance. Align yourself on all fours, hands beneath the shoulders and knees beneath the hips. Your spine is in neutral (see p.31). On an out breath, draw your pelvic floor and lower belly up and in. Breathe in to hold this position. As you breathe out, gently release. Repeat this 5 times.

Feet in parallel

Feet in Pilates stance

The Pilates stance

You'll find this position in many Pilates exercises, working the powerhouse (see p.37), buttock muscles, and inner thighs. Stand upright, spine in neutral (see p.31), arms down by your sides. Begin with the feet in parallel, toes and heels together. As you breathe out, open the feet. Keep the weight even through all 10 toes. Repeat this 5 times.

Careful! Never slump the spine forwards. It should feel active and lifted in this position. Relax the shoulders, elbows wide.

The seated C-curve

The C-curve requires the ability to scoop your abdominals (see p.32) without affecting the position of the spine, mobilizing the spine with control. Sit tall, with knees bent and legs hip-width apart. Place your hands behind your thighs. Breathe deeply into the back of your body. As you breathe out, scoop the abdominals, lifting the ribcage away from the hips, and curl your tailbone underneath to roll the spine into a C-shape. Your shoulders are in line with your hips. Repeat this 5 times.

The powerhouse

The powerhouse, a term coined by Joe Pilates (see p.10), refers to the core muscles (see p.19), plus strong mobilizing muscles, such as the six-pack abdominals, inner thighs, and buttocks. He also called it your "girdle of strength", a corset of muscles supporting the torso, stabilizing the body, and allowing power for movement. Here we learn to recruit the powerhouse, engaging the muscles appropriately and slowly, like a dimmer switch. Repeat 8 times. Stay soft and still in the spine as you engage the muscles.

Neck presses

This is a posture check that encourages length in your spine and relaxes the neck. Sit cross-legged on your mat, evenly on both sitting bones. Place the back of one hand on your forehead, with your other hand on top of it. Lengthen the crown of your head up towards the ceiling as you press the head into the hands, resisting the movement with your neck muscles. Don't allow the neck to move backwards. Hold for 2 breaths. Repeat 5 times.

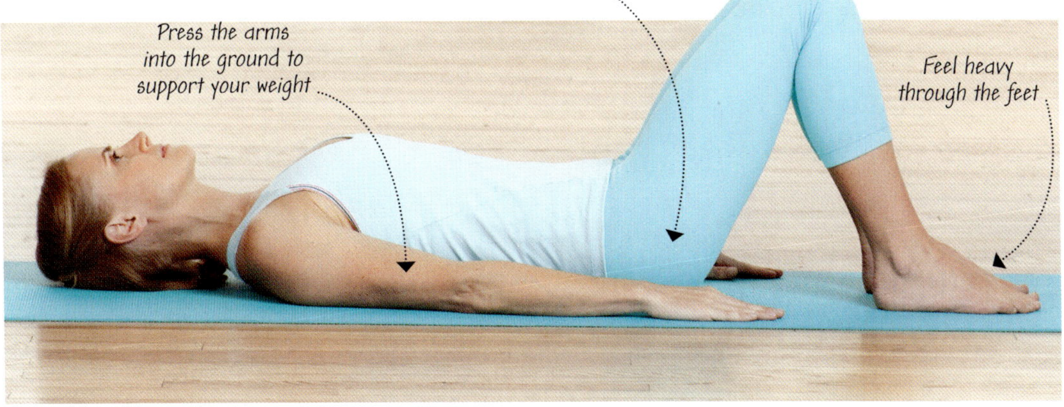

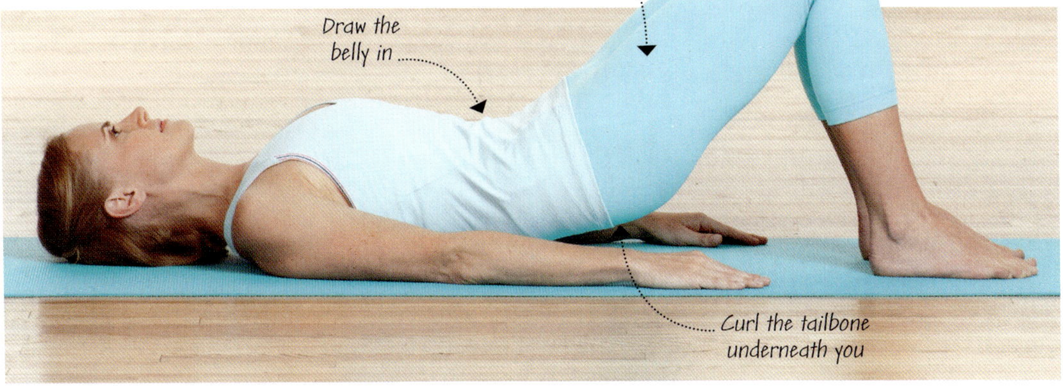

Pelvic curls

Focus on spinal alignment and the sequential mobility of the spine, moving evenly, bone by bone, like a wheel. Lie on your back with your feet flat on the floor, hip-width apart. Relax the head. Breathe in to prepare. As you breathe out, connect to your powerhouse and curl the tailbone under, releasing the lower spine into the mat. Then lift the buttocks to peel the spine off the floor slightly. Breathe in as you lower, slowly. Repeat 5 times.

Centring

Strengthen Core • **Practise** Control

This is a great way to strengthen your core (the muscles that protect your lower back, abdominals, and pelvic floor). Revisit it regularly to reinforce the feeling in your body and strengthen the connection to your powerhouse (see p.37).

1 Lie on your back with knees bent and feet flat on the floor. Release your body onto the floor with your breath. Relax the hips. Relax the shoulders and connect to your abdominals. Breathe in to prepare.

2 Breathe out and lengthen one arm back, simultaneously stretching the opposite leg forwards, in line with the body. Keep the spine long and still. Float the arm and leg back as you breathe in. Alternate sides. Repeat up to 8 times on each side.

More of a challenge

Stretch both arms and legs together. Hold your spine stable by scooping your belly deeply to anchor the torso. Keep your arms in line with the ears.

Careful! Don't allow your back to arch as you stretch.

Neck Peels

Strengthen Stomach • **Practise** Precision

This tones the abdominal muscles, while keeping the neck free from strain. Allow the weight of your head to be carried entirely by your arms and the band, not by the neck.

1 Lie centrally on top of a band or towel, placed underneath your tailbone and the entire length of the spine, with your feet flat on the floor. Soften the ribs towards the hips.

2 Breathe out, scoop your abdominals by drawing your waistline in and up, and gently peel the head and shoulder blades off the mat, feeling the head heavy on the band, and no strain in the neck. Breathe in at the top of the curl, and breathe out to release down slowly. Repeat 5 times.

Wall: Roll Down

Strengthen Stomach • **Practise** Flowing Movement

Roll downs challenge your abdominals by working against gravity to rebuild the spine sequentially. Resist the curl forwards by constantly lifting your belly.

1 Stand against the wall with your feet slightly away from the wall, in Pilates stance. Your spine should be neutral, neither arched nor tucked under.

Why? We use the belly muscles to support and mobilize the spine. It's important to learn how to recruit them correctly, working against gravity.

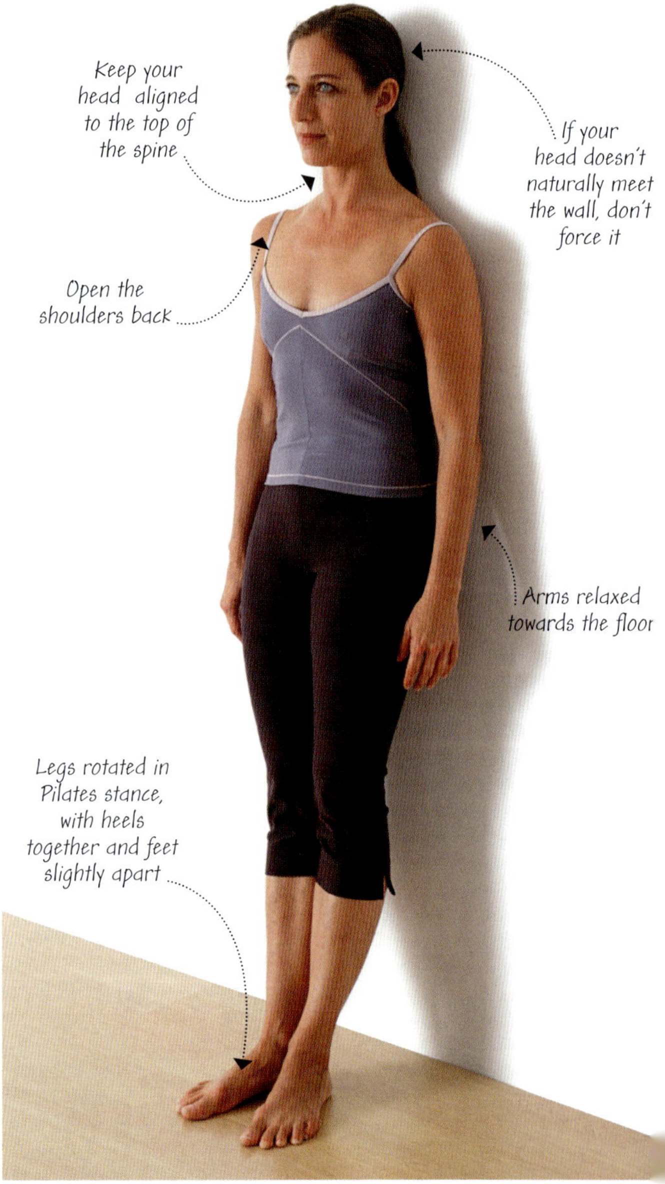

Take care...

If you feel a strain in your neck or shoulders, build the movement up slowly until you have released all tension. Learn to let go of your arms and neck completely.

Don't let your tailbone move up the wall. Be careful not to hinge at the hips. Keep the pelvis upright by scooping the abdominals.

Don't let your abdominals collapse forwards. Feel the movement coming from your centre, peeling the spine off the wall and then replacing it smoothly.

2 As you breathe out, scoop the belly, nod the nose down, and peel the spine from the wall: first the head, then the shoulders.

Imagine Peel the top of your spine away from the wall like a drooping flower, while the rest stays anchored and lifted.

Remember "Scoop your belly" means to hollow your abdominals up and in.

3 Roll the spine as far as you can without allowing the tailbone to rise up. Keep the pelvis upright. Breathe in. Then breathe out and re-stack the spine to standing, bone by bone. Repeat up to 10 times.

Imagine Draw the belly in really deeply, as if you're hanging over a washing line.

Wall: Stand

Strengthen Core • **Practise** Centring and Breathing

This is a fantastic posture check that you can do anywhere, any time: at home, at work, or at play. It's a great way to connect to your body.

Stand at the wall, with your feet slightly away and your legs in Pilates stance. Lean back, spine in neutral and head heavy into the wall. Scan your body: check your neck is released, your ribs are connected to your hips, and your lower back is long. Breathe wide and full into your back, and ensure you are connected to your centre. Repeat for as long as you need to relax your spine and centre your body.

Wall: Chair

Strengthen Arms and Legs • **Practise** Control

This move requires focus and strength, and uses weights to tone the arms. You'll feel your thighs burning! Avoid this exercise if you have knee problems.

1 Stand tall, with your feet hip-width apart. Place your feet slightly farther away from the wall than in Wall: Stand (see opposite). Hold the hand weights and relax your arms by your sides.

2 Breathe in. As you breathe out, slide your spine down the wall to "sit", with your knees directly over the ankles. Float the arms up to shoulder height, palms down. Hold for 5 breaths. Repeat, increasing the number of breaths each time, working up to 10. Breathe out as you slide back up, lowering the arms as you do so.

Wall: Circles

Strengthen Shoulders • **Practise** Flowing Movement

Here we learn to move the arms freely with control, while keeping the centre strong. You can also do this with hand weights for arm toning.

1 Stand against the wall, feet slightly away from the wall, shoulders wide. Float your arms forwards and up to shoulder height. Scoop the belly to support the lower back, feeling it releasing towards the wall, spine in neutral.

Imagine As you stand, imagine your neck lengthening away from rest of the spine, lifting the crown of the head up to the ceiling.

Take care...

If your neck feels tense, imagine the movement coming from the centre of the shoulder blades, floating the arms from your ribcage rather than from the neck.

Don't let your spine arch or tuck under – keep it in neutral. Keep the belly pulled in slightly and scooped.

Don't let your arms move at a different pace. Concentrate and control the movement, coordinating the movement of each arm in time with the other.

2 Open the arms out to the sides, keeping them in your peripheral vision. Keep the shoulders integrated into your body. Draw the abdominals deeper up and in.

Careful! Don't open your arms too wide or you will arch your back.

3 Float the arms down towards the hips once more. Keep the neck reaching up towards the ceiling, with your spine long and relaxed. Lower the arms to just in front of the hips. Repeat the circle 3 times in each direction, breathing naturally.

Biceps: Front Curls

Strengthen Arms • **Practise** Precision

These exercises are great for toning arms. Connect to your powerhouse and make this an all-body exercise. Imagine you're working under water to offer more resistance to your muscles.

1 Stand tall, in Pilates stance, holding a weight in each hand. Connect strongly from your heels up to the inner thighs and buttocks. Scoop the belly. Float the arms forwards to shoulder height, palms facing up. Keep the elbows unlocked.

2 Bend both arms in towards you, keeping the elbows level. Breathe in to bend the arms in, and out to lengthen them away. Repeat 5 times, working up to 10.

Careful! Don't tense the neck or lean back. Keep the shoulders away from the ears.

Biceps: Side Curls

Strengthen Arms • **Practise** Centring

Holding the arms out to the sides focuses on slightly different muscles. Here we tone the deltoids (shoulder muscles) as well as the biceps. Stay strongly connected to your centre throughout.

1 Float your arms out to the sides, in your peripheral vision, with your palms facing up. Keep your shoulders soft, ribs connected into the torso, belly deeply scooped.

Imagine As you move, imagine the crown of your head being lifted to the ceiling.

2 Curl the arms up, bending the elbows to about 90°. Relax the shoulders and keep the elbows level. Scoop in the belly deeply. Repeat 5 times, building up to 10. Breathe in to bend the arms in, and out to extend them away.

Boxing

Strengthen Arms • **Practise** Control

This tones and sculpts the arms and shoulders and requires a lot of core strength. Be strict with yourself and really control your movements, and you'll see results in no time.

1 Stand tall, with your feet hip-width apart and parallel. Bend the knees over the toes, scoop the belly, and hinge forwards, keeping the back long. Bend your arms upwards to bring the hands to the shoulders. Keep your elbows into your waist and feel your shoulder blades snug into your back. Breathe in to prepare.

Remember Stay soft and long in the neck, and keep the weight even on both feet.

2 As you breathe out, reach the right arm forwards and the left arm back, pressing the fists away. Breathe in to bring them back to centre. Repeat 3 sets. Roll the spine down and allow the arms to release towards the floor. Breathe out and roll the spine up, bone by bone, back to standing.

Careful! Try not to let your arms drop: they should reach in line with the shoulders. Keep the belly lifted and the shoulder blades connected into the back.

Standing Side Bends

Strengthen Waist • **Practise** Flowing Movement

This is a wonderful way to tone the oblique muscles in the waist, as well as the shoulders. Move smoothly, with control, and you'll soon see the results.

1 Stand in Pilates stance. Breathe in to lengthen the right arm up above you, in line with your ear. Draw the belly in and relax the neck. Keep the shoulder soft and away from the ear. Lift the crown of your head towards the ceiling. Plant your feet down into the ground.

2 Breathe out, reach the right arm up, and across to the left. Relax the left arm down by your side. Breathe in, feeling a stretch in the right side. Breathe out, return to centre, and lower the right arm. Repeat on the other side. Perform 6 repetitions.

Chest Expansion

Strengthen Arms and Upper Back • **Practise** Breathing

This is a great way to open the chest and work the muscles of the upper back, between the shoulder blades. Try to do this every day, to counteract a slumping posture.

1 Stand tall in Pilates stance, strongly engaging the inner thighs and buttocks. Float both arms in front of the body, palms down, shoulders relaxed.

Imagine As you exercise, imagine the crown of your head and neck extending to the ceiling. Direct your eyes down towards the floor, nodding the chin gently towards the chest.

Take care...

Don't arch your back. Keep your spine lengthened and stable as you move the arms. When you press the arms behind, draw deeper into your centre to make sure you resist the spine arching.

Try not to rock on your feet. Keep your weight evenly grounded through the feet as you move the arms. Stay connected with the legs and spread the weight through all 10 toes and your heels.

The body shouldn't twist with the head. Make sure this is a movement just in the neck, free from the torso.

2 Breathe in, and press your arms back, feeling the triceps activate as you reach the arms behind you. Feel the shoulder blades drawing inwards.

Careful! Avoid arching the back. Keep your waist long and belly lifted.

3 Look over the right shoulder, then the left. Return to centre. Breathe out to glide the arms back to the front of the body. Repeat, alternating your gaze, turning your head from left to right, then right to left. Repeat each set 3 times, trying to open the chest more every time.

Hundred Preparation

Strengthen Stomach • **Practise** Breathing

This tough exercise may not become your favourite, but it is very effective. This is a classic breathing exercise in Pilates, and targets the deep abdominals.

1 Sit tall, feet hip-width apart. Hold behind your thighs lightly. Draw the abdominals in and up. Breathe in. As you breathe out, curl the tailbone under and begin to roll down onto the mat.

Why? Breathing fully and moving on the out breath helps to engage the abdominals strongly. Breathing into the back of the ribcage is the only way to perform this exercise smoothly and correctly.

Take care...

Don't let your feet lift. Keep the feet heavy and grounded into the floor, allow this to help you connect to your abdominals.

Your body shouldn't move as the arms pump freely. Keep your scoop strong and make sure the spine doesn't move.

Try not to tilt your head back. Keep the eyes focused in towards your navel and the neck long.

2 Curl down with control, keeping the eyes focused forwards, not up. Engage your abdominals to release the lower spine towards the mat. Keep the upper body curled off the mat and the chest open.

3 Release the arms forwards. Breathe in and pump the arms for 5 counts, then breathe out and pump for 5 counts. Continue pumping until you reach 50. Breathe out and roll back up to sitting.

Tip Pump the arms down towards the floor and up towards the knees, as if you are bobbing a ball underneath. Your shoulders should move freely in the joints and the arms should move as one unbroken unit from shoulder to fingertip. Don't allow the hands to flop or bend the wrists or elbows.

Roll Back

Strengthen Stomach • **Practise** Control

This exercise requires a deep connection to your powerhouse to help you move. Check this connection throughout the exercise so you don't let it slip. It's great practice for more advanced work.

1 Sit tall, with the feet grounded and hip-width apart. Place your hands lightly under your thighs. Scoop your belly and lengthen your waist. Breathe in to prepare.

Imagine To keep your waist long, imagine you have elastic bands connecting your ribs down towards your hips. Try to keep the bands taut; don't allow them to expand and lose the connection.

Take care...

Don't hinge from the hip. The movement should be a rolling C-curve from the tailbone, and not straight from the upper back.

Avoid arching the back and allowing the ribs to pop forwards. Keep the abdominals strong.

Don't look up to the ceiling. Keep the neck long and eyes focused towards your centre.

2 Breathe out, deepen your abdominals, and curl the tailbone underneath to roll your lower back towards the mat. Nod the chin to the chest to finish the C-curve of the spine.

3 Scoop more and release the mid-back into the mat. Hold this position for 3 breaths. As you breathe out each time, pull your belly in more. Keep the deep engagement to roll the spine back up to the sitting position, on an out breath. Repeat 3 times.

Careful! Keep the waist long on both sides. Think about your box and try not to collapse on one side.

Roll Up

Strengthen Stomach • **Practise** Control and Breathing

This wonderful exercise works on your strength, flexibility, and control. We move the spine sequentially, rolling each part evenly like a wheel, using the abdominals strongly.

1 Lie flat on the mat and lengthen your arms overhead, in line with your ears. Connect the ribs down. Squeeze your inner thighs and flex your feet.

Remember All the principles of Pilates are illustrated in this exercise, and your body will feel the effects if you take the time to perfect the movement.

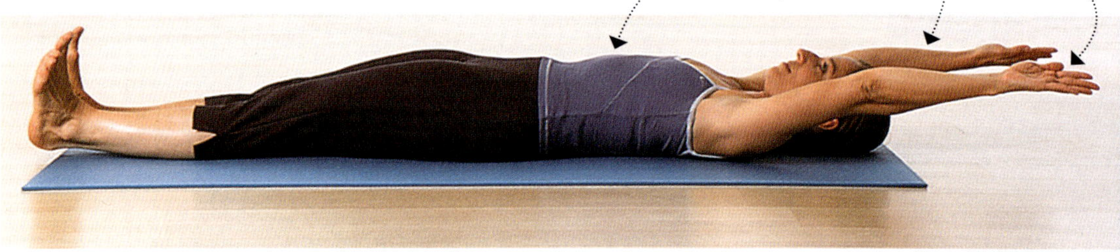

2 Breathe in; float the arms above the shoulders. Nod the chin towards the chest; look down towards your centre. Scoop the belly deeply and flex the feet.

3 Breathe out and curl the upper body off the mat, lifting the ribs and deepening the abdominals. Press the arms forwards and towards the toes.

Imagine Think of your spine as a string of pearls: you're picking the pearls up one by one, then smoothly laying them down again.

4 Breathe in; draw the belly in as you roll forwards over your legs, reaching the arms to your toes. Breathe out to roll the spine back down to the mat, bone by bone. As your shoulders meet the mat, reach the arms back behind you. Repeat the exercise 5 times.

Make it easier

If you can't control the movement, bend the knees slightly and place your hands under your thighs to help you support yourself while you build strength. Move slowly through each part of the spine.

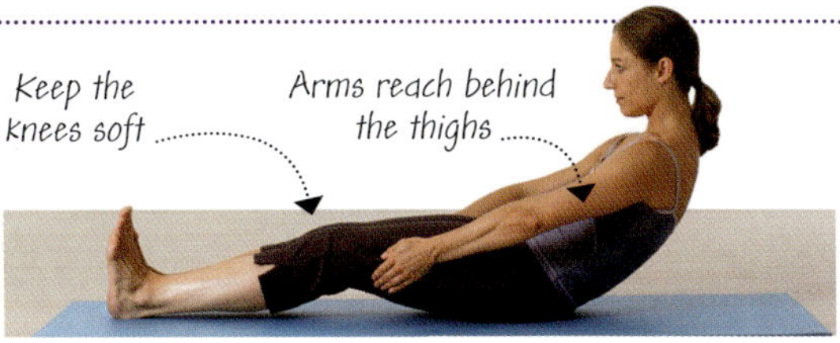

Leg Circles

Strengthen Thighs and Buttocks

Practise Concentration and Precision

It takes a lot of control to ensure there is no unwanted movement in the body. Use your powerhouse (see p.37) in this exercise to anchor the torso while the legs move.

1 Lying on the mat, align yourself centrally on your back, with one leg bent and the other extended up in the air, in line with the hip. Scoop the belly. Relax the spine into neutral.

Remember The purpose of this exercise is to control your movement, so keep your torso stable and use your abdominals for control.

Side view

2 Connect to your centre and sweep the extended leg across the body, using the inner thigh muscles. Aim the big toe towards your opposite shoulder.

3 Circle the leg down and around, and back up to centre. Breathe in for the first half of the circle, out for the second. Repeat 8 times in each direction. Make the circles precise and even.

Why? Leg circles encourage freedom of movement without affecting a strong core. In Pilates, isolating certain parts – like the thighs and buttocks here – ensures your muscles are balanced and no tension is introduced anywhere.

Rolling Like a Ball 1

Strengthen Stomach • **Practise** Flowing Movement

This playful exercise is surprisingly challenging for your core. Work hard to maintain your C-curve for a smooth and flowing movement. Practise it swiftly, for flow, and slowly, to develop your concentration and control.

1 Sit tall on your mat. Hold the backs of the thighs lightly. Use your abdominals to float your legs up, shins parallel with the floor, tipping back off your sitting bones. Curl into a C-curve (see p.36) and balance for a moment to prepare.

Imagine Think of a ball encircling your body, so when you roll back, you roll smoothly and continuously.

2 Breathe in and roll back smoothly. As you roll to your shoulder blades, maintain your body shape and lengthen your tailbone to the ceiling. Stay long in the neck and relaxed in the shoulders, keeping the belly strong to make sure your spine doesn't straighten.

Careful! Don't roll too far. Roll only as far as the shoulders: the head should not touch the floor.

3 Breathe out, deepen your scoop, and roll forwards, to balance once more. Practise slowly with control until your C-curve is perfect, then build up to a swift movement for more strength. Synchronize your movement to your breath. The out breath will give you the momentum to roll forwards. Repeat 6–8 times.

Imagine Think of yourself as a pendulum, rocking easily and swiftly. Try to create that sense of rhythm as you roll, controlled but flowing.

Take care...

Don't tilt your head back. If the eye-focus floats to the ceiling, the head will rock back. Keep your eyes focused into your centre, chin nodding towards the chest.

Don't lose the C-curve and flatten the spine. Keep the abdominals constantly scooping in more deeply to strengthen the C-curve throughout the movement.

What not to do

Single Leg Stretch 1

Strengthen Stomach and Thighs

Practise Flowing Movement and Concentration

This is one of the most effective tummy-toning exercises you can do. Focus on alignment and control, as you flow swiftly from a strong centre.

1 Lie in the centre of your mat. Float your knees into your chest and take your hands around your right knee. Breathe in and curl your head and shoulders off the mat, simultaneously reaching your left leg away.

Tip To help you keep the curl-up position, aim your gaze between your thighs, belly deeply scooped. Do not lose the curl-up.

2 As you breathe out, draw the leg in and switch the arm and leg positions. Breathe in to extend the left leg, and out to extend the right leg. Repeat up to 8 times on each leg.

Careful! Stay central and keep the torso controlled. Think about your box (see p.30).

Take care...

Don't drop your head back so your eye-focus floats up. This places strain on the neck. Keep the eyes focused down towards the pelvis.

Make sure your head is centred on the spine as the limbs move. The head should remain still: think of your box square and even.

Try not to collapse the knee into the chest. Keep it precise.

What not to do

Double Leg Stretch 1

Strengthen Stomach and Buttocks • **Practise** Centring

Lengthening your limbs away from your centre is a real test of your core strength and control. Keep in mind all the Pilates principles – this exercise will really challenge you.

1 Lie on your back, float your knees into your chest and hug them in using your hands. On an out breath, curl your head towards your knees.

Tip Draw in your belly, scooping it away from your nose. Keep the shoulders relaxed.

2 Breathe in and reach your arms forwards. Check that your scoop stays deep and the lower back sinks towards the mat.

Help! If your neck strains, take one hand behind your head.

3 Reach your legs away. Squeeze the inner thighs and deepen your scoop. Breathe out, hug the knees in, then repeat without curling back down. Repeat 6–8 times.

Careful! Don't allow the back to arch. Take the legs only as low as you can control them.

Spine Stretch Forwards 1

Strengthen Back and Stomach • **Practise** Breathing

This will test your C-curve (see p.36) and strengthen the abdominals and the spine. It's also a wonderful way of stretching the back and hamstrings, and making you aware of your posture.

1 Sit tall, with your legs lengthened, slightly wider than hip-width apart. Press your hands into the mat, in between your legs. Feel your shoulder blades soften back. Lengthen the ribcage up, away from the hips.

Tip Check the entire body is active and you'll feel the exercise more effectively. Press out through the feet and feel the crown of the head lengthen upwards. Imagine your spine is like a spring, reaching and stretching.

2 As you breathe out, nod the chin to the chest, and curl your spine into a C-curve. Nod the crown of the head forwards. Hold the arches of the feet. Breathe in and stretch the spine and legs. As you breathe out, slowly re-stack the spine, using your abdominals. Press the palms into the floor once more. Repeat up to 5 times. Stay lifted in the abdominals and waist. Sit taller as you re-stack to an upright position.

Imagine As you pull forwards towards your feet, imagine there is a belt pulling your waist back.

Spine Twist

Strengthen Waist and Spine • **Practise** Precision

This exercise requires precision and control. The muscles on both sides of the body are equally challenged to produce the twisting movement, therefore toning the waist.

1 Sit tall, legs connected, hands clasped behind your head. Press out through the heels and draw the belly up and in. Breathe in and lengthen the spine.

Imagine To keep your back straight, imagine sitting tall with your spine lined up against a pole.

2 Breathe out and twist the spine to the right, keeping the pelvis square. Lift up through the crown of the head. Reach your left elbow forwards and the right elbow backwards, keeping the chest open.

Imagine As you twist, think of the ribcage spiralling around the spine, growing taller as you twist.

3 Breathe in to return to the centre, then breathe out to twist to the other side. Repeat 6 times on each side.

Tip Keep the spine lifting tall as you twist and the muscles will have to work harder. Imagine sending the ribcage back behind you, keeping the elbows wide.

1 2 3

Tick Tock

Strengthen Waist and Inner Thighs
Practise Control and Concentration

Control this movement and your abdominals will soon be well toned. Move slowly at first, gradually increasing the range until you can reach the legs lower with control.

1 Lie flat, fold your knees in, and lengthen the legs up to the ceiling, directly above the hips. Bring the legs into Pilates stance. Reach your arms out by your sides, pressing them into the floor to help ground the torso. Breathe in to prepare.

Help! If your legs cramp at 90°, bend the knees slightly.

2 Breathe out and lower the legs to the right. Ensure the legs are connected from the inner thighs to the heels. Feel the left side of your ribcage anchoring into the floor as the hips twist to the right. Breathe out to draw the legs back to centre. Then breathe in to lower the legs to the left. Repeat up to 5 times on each side.

Tip Feel this twist coming from your navel, not from your hips. Go only as low as you can control with your abdominals.

Swan Preparation

Strengthen Back • **Practise** Precision

This is a great way to counteract bad posture. It opens out the chest and strengthens the muscles of the mid-back and of the upper arms.

1 Lie on your front, with legs together in parallel. Place the hands directly beneath the shoulders and draw the elbows in tightly to the waist, pointing them back, as if you're a crocodile.

Careful! Try not to sink into and compress the lower back. Always keep the stomach muscles lifted.

2 Breathe in. As you breathe out, look up, glide the shoulder blades back, and open your chest up. Push the elbows down towards the floor. Hold for 5 breaths, keeping the belly lifted. Breathe out and lower down to the mat slowly. Repeat 5 times.

Tip Activate the muscles in between the shoulder blades to lift the spine. Keep the neck long, throat open.

Knee Stretches

Strengthen Stomach and Buttocks
Practise Control and Flowing Movement

Great for coordination and control, this exercise combines flowing movement of the spine with reaching limbs away from a strong centre. It's a great way to focus your mind on your body.

1 Come onto all fours in the centre of your mat. Think about your Pilates box, with long waist even on both sides. Draw the belly up away from the floor. Lengthen the spine into neutral. Spread the weight evenly through the hands. Breathe in to prepare.

Imagine Visualize yourself as a table, strong and sturdy, with your weight supported evenly through each limb.

2 As you breathe out, curl the tailbone underneath you and roll the spine up into a C-curve. Simultaneously, bring the right knee in towards your forehead. Keep the belly lifted.

Careful! Try to stay centred on your mat. Try not to allow the body to lean and wobble as you move the leg. Stay strong and centred.

3 Breathe in and lengthen the right leg back behind you, keeping your hips square. Extend the spine and bring your gaze up. Increase the momentum and repeat 6–8 times on the right side, then shift to the left leg and perform the same number of repetitions.

Remember Alignment is key. Try not to allow the body to rock from side to side. Keep your box still as the leg reaches away.

Take care...

Don't take your leg up too high. Make sure you control the movement and keep the leg in line with the hip. Lifting too high will allow the back to arch.

Don't rock your body from side to side. Keep your core strong and stay central on your mat.

The opposite hip shouldn't drop as you bring the leg in. Use your powerhouse to stay level in the hips.

Increase the momentum gradually and always more precisely. Try not to swing your whole body with the leg. Keep the abdominals strong to control the movement.

Side Kicks: Front 1

Strengthen Waist and Buttocks • **Practise** Centring

This tones the waist and buttocks, challenging your balance and control. When performing the Side Kick series (see pp.72–75), repeat all exercises on one side before rolling over and repeating the entire sequence on the other side.

1 Lie down on your side, legs straight and at about 45°, hips and shoulders stacked on top of each other. Scoop the belly in, lengthening the waist. Rest your head on your hand. Place your top hand on the mat in front of your ribcage.

Tip Release the arm and rest it on the floor, and relax your head onto your arm.

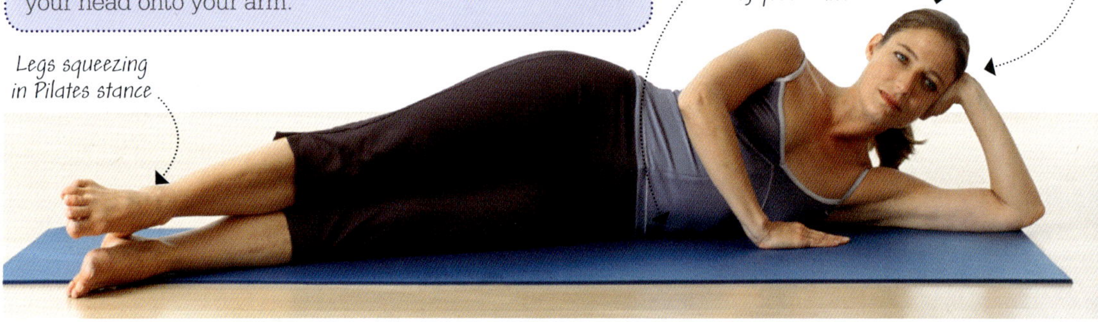

2 Breathe out, lift the top leg, in line with the hip. Keep the waist long and belly deeply scooped. Try to make the top leg longer than the bottom leg, and remember to move with length.

3 Breathe in and swing your leg forwards, then pulse forwards twice by pushing your leg forwards and back a little bit more in small, heartbeat movements. Ensure the tailbone doesn't curl forwards with the thighbone. Keep the leg lifted and parallel with the floor.

Imagine Visualize sliding your leg along a table, staying on exactly the same level throughout.

Take care...

Don't swing your spine with the leg. Make sure your bottom doesn't curl under as the leg comes forwards. Keep your core strong so the spine is stable and resists movement.

4 Breathe out, sweep the top leg back, opening the front of the hip. Make sure the knee doesn't bend. Repeat 6–8 times on this side, then roll over and repeat on the other side.

Careful! Make sure the spine doesn't swing with the leg. Keep your powerhouse working.

1 2 3

Side Kicks: Double Leg Lift

Strengthen Inner Thighs, Buttocks, and Waist
Practise Precision

Working your waist and thighs, this adds a little more challenge to your Side Kick series. Think about balance and control, as well as the precision and pacing of the movement.

1 Lie on your side with your legs forwards by about 45°. Use the mat as a guide for your alignment. Lengthen your feet towards the front of the mat. Place the legs in the Pilates stance. Breathe in.

Tip Focus on length, reaching the legs away from the crown of the head. Keep the abdominals working hard.

2 Breathe out, lift and lengthen both legs up, with inner thighs squeezing and reaching away through the toes. Breathe in. Breathe out and release the legs down slowly. Repeat up to 8 times on each side.

Tip Lift the legs only as high as you can.

Side Kicks: Lower Lift

Strengthen Core • **Practise** Concentration

Concentrate on your alignment and coordination for this exercise, working the targeted areas while keeping the rest of your body long and free from tension.

1 Lie on your mat. Breathe in to prepare and lengthen your spine. Keep the waist long on both sides and strongly engage the belly muscles. Breathe out to lift both legs together, squeezing the buttocks and thighs.

Tip Keep the waist long to avoid slumping into the mat.

2 Breathe in and lower the bottom leg towards the floor, then breathe out to lift it again, squeezing the inner thighs and heels. Lift and lower up to 10 times, lifting with the out breath and deepening the abdominals. Release both legs down together. Repeat up to 8 times.

Mermaid

Strengthen Waist and Core
Practise Centring and Flowing Movement

This is a lovely stretch after the Side Kicks series – to stretch the waist – creating space in your spine and working on flow.

1 Sit tall with your legs curled to one side and knees level. Try to feel evenly grounded through both the sitting bones and lifted through your waist. Breathe in and float one arm up in line with the ear, and take the other around the shins. Think about lifting your ribcage up and away from the hips throughout. Stay square and try not to allow the box to collapse.

Careful! If you have knee problems, you need to avoid this exercise because it might put pressure on the knee joints.

2 Breathe out; reach the arm up and over the body, lengthening both sides of the waist. Breathe in to use your powerhouse.

Imagine As you reach your arm up, imagine you are painting a line on the ceiling above you with your fingertips.

Careful! Make sure you don't collapse the bottom side of the waist. The obliques should lift the ribcage throughout.

3 Float back to the centre with your out breath. Lengthen the spine and relax the shoulders. Keep your gaze forwards to ensure the head is in line with the spine; don't tilt the head down.

Tip Feel the spine lifting up before it bends. Create a space between each vertebra.

4 Breathe out to place the arm down onto the mat, bending the elbow. Float the other arm up and across. Repeat 3 times on each side. The legs remain still and anchored as the body floats gracefully as if under water.

Remember It should be a graceful, flowing movement. Stay lifted in the waist throughout.

Take care...

Don't collapse your chest. Keep the shoulders open, as if you are sliding between two panes of glass.

Don't keep your eyes focused downwards. Make sure you look straight ahead throughout the movement and keep the neck in line with the spine.

What not to do

Shoulder Bridge

Strengthen Buttocks and Core • **Practise** Control

This exercise tones the buttocks and builds your strength and stamina. Imagine you are under water and use the resistance to make your movements precise. Hold the pelvis lifted and stable, as you move the legs with control.

1 Lie on your back with your arms relaxed by your sides. Your legs are hip-width apart, feet flat on the floor. Your spine is in neutral, powerhouse engaged. Breathe in to prepare.

2 Breathe out and hinge the hips up in one movement. Keep the ribcage connected to avoid arching the back. Shoulders are heavy and open, arms pressing into the floor. Hold this position for 5 breaths. Release the spine back down, then move on to step 3.

3 Hinge the hips up once again. Extend your right leg up to the ceiling, foot softly pointed. Make sure your hips stay level and lifted, your box strong. Feel heavy and grounded through the supporting foot.

4 Breathe in and kick the leg down, flexing the foot. Repeat steps 3 and 4 five times. Breathe out for up-kick and in for down-kick, then float the foot down, keeping the hips lifted. Repeat with the other leg.

Take care...

Don't drop the hips on one side. Think about your box and keep it square and lifted.

Don't lift the shoulders. Keep your shoulders released heavily into the floor.

Check your foot isn't too close to your bottom. Keep it in line with the knee, so the spine can lengthen.

What not to do

15-Minute Sequence

1 Pilates Stance
p.35

2 Wall: Roll Down
pp.42–43

3 Standing Side Bends
p.51

6 Leg Circles
pp.60–61

7 Rolling Like a Ball 1
pp.62–63

10 Spine Stretch Forwards 1
p.66

11 Spine Twist
p.67

4 Hundred Preparation
pp.54–55

5 Roll Back
pp.56–57

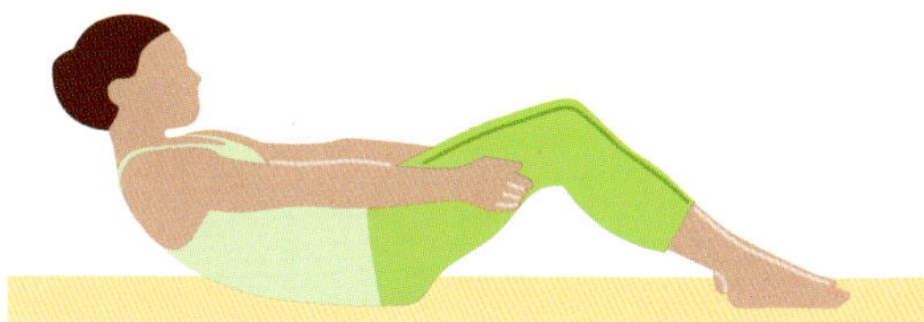

8 Single Leg Stretch 1
p.64

9 Double Leg Stretch 1
p.65

12 Swan Preparation
p.69

13 Mermaid
p.76–77

30-Minute Sequence

1 Pilates Stance
p.35

2 Wall: Roll Down
p.42

3 Wall: Stand
p.44

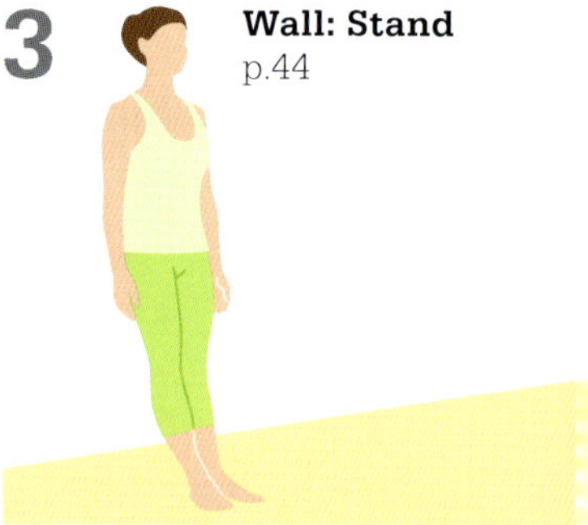

7 Pelvic Curls
p.39

8 Hundred Preparation
pp.54–55

9 Roll Back
pp.56–57

13 Single Leg Stretch 1
p.64

14 Double Leg Stretch 1
p.65

15 Spine Stretch Forwards 1
p.66

19 Swan Preparation
p.69

20 Mermaid
pp.76–77

4 Wall: Chair
p.45

5 Standing Side Bends
p.51

6 Neck Presses
p.38

10 Roll Up
pp.58–59

11 Leg Circles
pp.60–61

12 Rolling Like a Ball 1
pp.62–63

16 Spine Twist
p.67

17 Knee Stretches
pp.70–71

18 Side Kicks: Front 1
pp.72–73

45-Minute Sequence

1
Pilates Stance
p.35

2 **Wall: Roll Down**
p.42

3 **Wall: Stand**
p.44

7 **Neck Presses**
p.38

8 **Pelvic Curls**
p.39

9 **Seated C-curve**
p.36

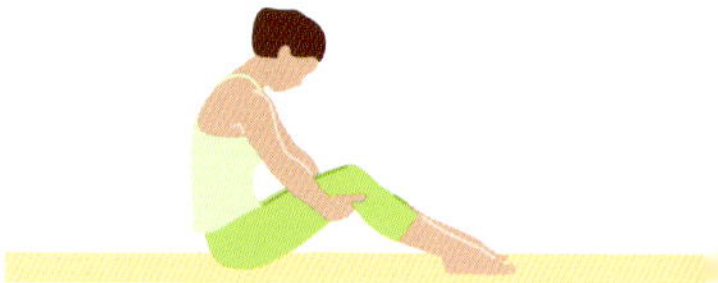

13 **Leg Circles**
pp.60–61

14 **Rolling Like a Ball 1**
pp.62–63

15 **Single Leg Stretch 1**
p.64

19 **Knee Stretches**
pp.70–71

20 **Side Kicks: Front 1**
p.72–73

21 **Side Kicks: Double Leg Lift**
p.74

25 **Swan Preparation**
p.69

26 **Mermaid**
p.76–77

27
Wall: Circles
pp.46–47

4 **Wall: Chair** p.45

5 **Standing Side Bends** p.51

6 **Powerhouse** p.37

10 **Hundred Preparation** pp.54–55

11 **Roll Back** pp.56–57

12 **Roll Up** pp.58–59

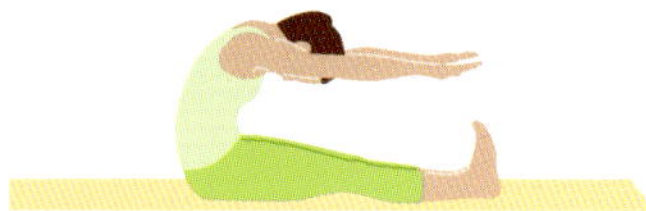

16 **Double Leg Stretch 1** p.65

17 **Spine Stretch Forwards 1** p.66

18 **Spine Twist** p.67

22 **Side Kicks: Lower Lift** p.75

23 **Tick Tock** p.68

24 **Shoulder Bridge** pp.78–79

28 **Biceps: Front Curls** p.48

29 **Biceps: Side Curls** p.49

30 **Boxing** p.50

Assess your progress

How did you progress over the last six weeks? Go back and check your baselines (see pp.28–29). How do you feel compared to the first time you performed the exercises? Did you notice an improvement? If so, well done! Keep at it!

Common problems

Did you make less progress than you'd hoped? Don't be disheartened. Look again at the sections on The 6 Principles of Pilates (see pp.8–11) and Key Techniques (see pp.30–39). Practise, practise, practise any key techniques that still don't make sense to you. Be honest: did you stick to the programme and focus on each detail fully as you worked? Pilates is all about detail, so your progress directly reflects the effort and concentration you put into each workout. Here are some common problems that beginners face.

"My muscles quiver when I curl up from the mat or hold my legs in the air."

This is not unusual. My Pilates teacher called it "the tremor of truth"! It means your muscles are working hard. As long as you don't feel any strain or sharp pain, breathe through the wobbling; your muscles will soon respond and strengthen. Deepen the abdominal connection as you curl up or move the limbs. Relax rather than tense up.

"I find it hard to arch my back up from the mat."

Being unable to lengthen the spine up from a face-down position, such as in Swan Preparation (see p.69), shows a lack of spinal flexibility. It is very common for bad posture to cause weak spinal muscles. To encourage more mobility, focus on practising this lying position, even if it feels uncomfortable (although never work through pain). Try to achieve even a small bending movement of the upper spine and aim to improve each time. Your mobility should increase, to benefit your posture and spinal health.

"My neck aches during the curl-up exercises."

Check your eye focus during these exercises. When abdominals tire, often you slightly lose your curl up and the head begins to drop back, so the eyes focus on the ceiling. This strains the neck muscles, causing an ache. Relax the head down whenever you feel this ache. To avoid it, deepen your powerhouse connection (see p.37). Make sure that your belly stays strong to the end of an exercise and keep your eyes focused towards your centre to keep the neck free and long.

"I can't straighten my legs."

Tight muscles respond very well to regular stretching. Continue with the programme: soften your knees if it is uncomfortable, but try to push yourself slightly to straighten a little farther each time. Your hamstrings will soon begin to lengthen.

"Pilates is too easy! This is boring."

Quite simply, if you find Pilates easy you are not working hard enough. Even the key techniques can offer as much challenge as you wish to take from them, so make the most of each exercise. Strive to perform each one precisely. Don't rush, really feel it: work slowly, with control, thinking about precision, lengthening, breathing, alignment, scoop, and coordination....

Assess your achievement

Didn't achieve your goals? Don't allow it to dampen your enthusiasm as you move to the next section (see pp.88–139). Celebrate every achievement as you practise, for example being able to coordinate your movement to your breath, or to straighten your leg slightly farther than before. Small results accumulate: soon you'll be setting yourself new goals.

Challenging exercises

Here is a plan to help you during your workouts over the next six weeks. At the end of the six weeks, look back over these goals and assess how you have progressed.

Goal: Control
Roll Back (see pp.56–57)

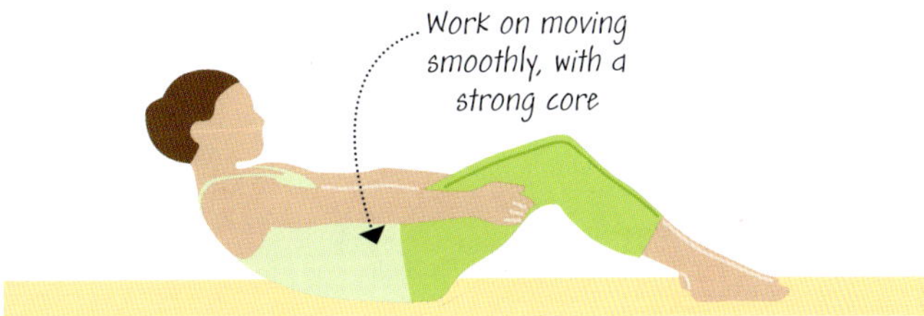

Goal: Centring
Centring (see p.40)

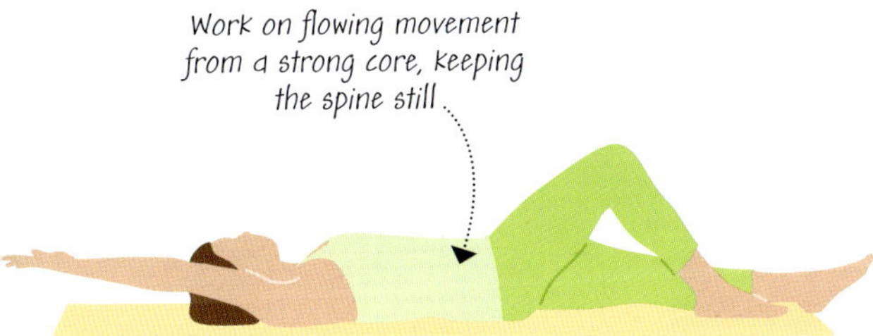

Goal: Flexibility
Wall: Roll Down (see pp.42–43)

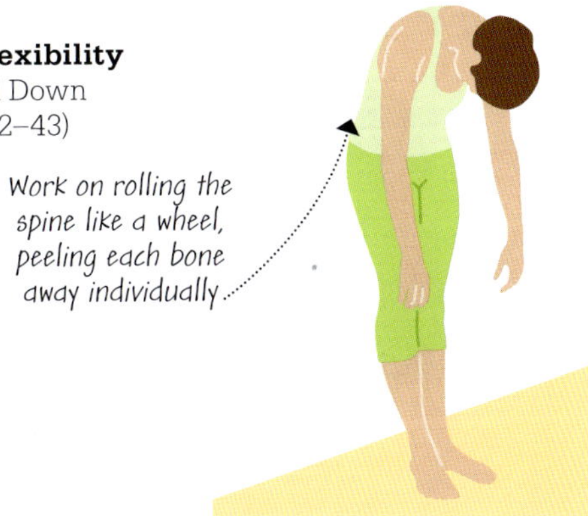

Goal: Strength
Wall: Chair (see p.45), Hundred Preparation (see pp.54–55), Roll Up (see pp.58–59)

Goal: Flowing Movement
Single Leg Stretch 1 (see p.64)

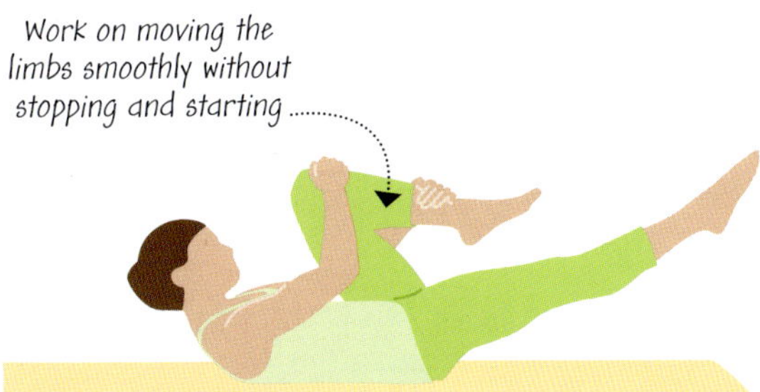

2

Build On It

Now that you've mastered the basics, you're ready to move on to more complex versions of some of the exercises, as well as some new ones. Continue to perfect the movements you already know and practise anything that you find challenging until you feel completely confident with each movement. Precision and concentration are key. After working through this chapter, you should find that you are performing the movement sequences in the exercise programme with much more fluidity and control.

Plan Your Programme

Well done for getting this far! By now you should feel stronger, more supple, and better coordinated. You may also feel that Pilates is becoming a part of your life and that you no longer have to think twice about scheduling workout time.

Planning the next step

Now we want to take the next steps into developing greater understanding of Pilates and really working our bodies harder to reach new goals with our newly acquired skills. Let's continue to use broadly the same goals as for the first stage, so that we can gain a real picture of how far we have come when we reach the end of this programme. Once you have followed these sequences for a few times, you could mix and match other exercises from the rest of the section – but take care to substitute any with an exercise that trains the same area of the body, to ensure that your workout remains balanced.

Build On It Exercise Programme

Use this specially designed Pilates exercise programme (below and opposite) to set yourself goals and assess your progress over the next six weeks. You can find summaries of the sequences on pp.132–137. Each week, when you work out, follow the sequence provided in this programme at least for the first few times, before you experiment with using other exercises on the same level. Remember to act as your own coach and don't allow yourself to be lazy or cheat – you will improve quicker if you perform every movement to the best of your ability.

Week 1: Focus on Alignment

Baseline: The original photographs you took at the start of the Start Simple Exercise Programme (see pp.28–29).

- **Day 1:** 15-minute sequence, check control, breathing

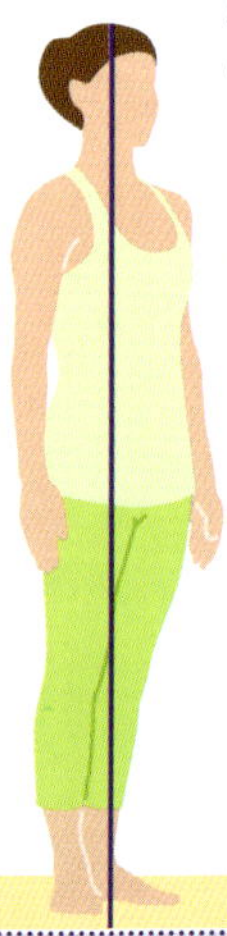

- **Day 2:** 30-minute sequence, check lengthening, stability
- **Day 3:** 45-minute sequence, check precision, control
- **Day 4:** 15-minute sequence, check stability, coordination.

Goal: take new photos after six weeks to see how much closer you are to ideal alignment.

Week 2: Focus on Control

Baseline: Perform the Teaser with Twist (see pp.126–127). Do you feel stiff and wobbly? Can you hold the position without shaking or tensing? Do you collapse in the spine or can you maintain length and height as you twist?

- **Day 1:** 15-minute sequence, check centring, alignment
- **Day 2:** 45-minute sequence, check concentration, precision
- **Day 3:** 15-minute sequence, check precision, breathing
- **Day 4:** 45-minute sequence, check flowing movement, stability.

Goal: do the exercise with control, precision, and fluidity, feeling strong and supported as you twist.

Week 3: Focus on Centring

Baseline: Perform Double Leg Stretch 2 (see pp.102–103). Does your spine arch as you lengthen the limbs away? Are the shoulders away from the ears? Is the spine supported and strong or does the lower back feel weak?

- **Day 1:** 15-minute sequence, check Pilates box, alignment, flowing movement
- **Day 2:** 30-minute sequence, check stability, precision, lengthening
- **Day 3:** 45-minute sequence, check precision, control, breathing
- **Day 4:** 30-minute sequence, check control, alignment.

Goal: a strong centre as you lengthen the limbs away, with no movement in the spine.

Week 4: Focus on Flexibility

Baseline: perform Single Straight Leg Stretch (see p.101). Are you able to straighten your legs up to the ceiling?

- **Day 1:** 15-minute sequence, check precision, control, alignment
- **Day 2:** 45-minute sequence, check breathing, scoop, stability
- **Day 3:** 45-minute sequence, check scoop, powerhouse, coordination
- **Day 4:** 30-minute sequence, check control, concentration.

Goal: lengthen and straighten the legs without wobbling.

Week 5: Focus on Strength

Baseline: try performing Ten by Ten (see pp.92–93), Half Roll Up (see pp.94–95), Teaser Preparation (see pp.124–125) without a break. On a scale of 1–10, how hard was each exercise and the sequence?

- **Day 1:** 15-minute sequence, check centring, control, coordination
- **Day 2:** 45-minute sequence, check scoop, alignment, concentration
- **Day 3:** 30-minute sequence, check alignment, coordination, flowing movement
- **Day 4:** 45-minute sequence, check control, precision, powerhouse.

Goal: when you do the sequence again, it should feel easier.

Week 6: Focus on Flowing Movement

Baseline: try Swimming (see pp.128–129). Does the movement feel fluid and controlled or jerky? Can you link leg and arm movements simultaneously without stopping the flow?

- **Day 1:** 30-minute sequence, check centring, breathing, coordination
- **Day 2:** 45-minute sequence, check stability, control, Pilates box
- **Day 3:** 30-minute sequence, check alignment, precision, coordination
- **Day 4:** 45-minute sequence, check precision, centring, breathing

Goal: make the movement smoother and swifter without wobbling or stopping.

Check your new baseline for each area of the body before you begin this exercise programme and make a note of how it feels to do each movement. Then, at the end of the six weeks, assess yourself, according to the goals given here, to see how far you have gone towards achieving your targets. Enjoy the next six weeks!

Ten by Ten

Strengthen Stomach • **Practise** Breathing

This exercise builds your strength for the full Hundred (see p.144). It warms up the body, works the powerhouse, and uses the Pilates breath wide into the back of the body. It should appear effortless, not laboured, as you work the muscles hard.

1 Sit tall, with your knees connected, feet flat on the floor. Reach your arms out in front, shoulders soft into your back. Breathe out to scoop the belly, curl the tailbone under, and begin to release the spine, bone by bone, into the mat. Maintain a strong engagement of your abdominals.

Tip Relax the shoulders and keep them connected into your body as your arms reach away.

2 Release down until you reach the tips of your shoulder blades. Your spine is curled, arms reaching away parallel with your thighs. Lengthen the right leg away from the knee, keeping the inner thighs parallel and glued together. Press the supporting foot into the ground. Squeeze deeply into the belly to keep stable.

Careful! As you reach the leg away, deepen the scoop of your belly and keep the spine lifted. Try not to collapse your form.

3 Extend the left leg to meet the right. Breathe in and pump the arms up and down – breathe in for 5 pumps and breathe out for 5. Then remain still and strong to breathe in for a count of 5 and out for 5. Alternate pumping and remaining still, continuing to breathe and pump in sets of 5 until you've reached 100.

Tip Feel light in the spine and move freely in the shoulder joints. Deepen the abdominals and imagine the rest of your body is serene as you dynamically pump the arms.

Take care...

Your neck shouldn't feel too strained. Your abdominals will get fatigued and need to be activated constantly. Keep your curl deep and powerhouse connected.

Don't move your torso. Move your shoulder joints without rocking the spine forwards and back. Turn up your powerhouse engagement to keep the spine still.

Arms and hands shouldn't be floppy. Keep arms strong and straight from shoulder to fingertips. The pump is from the shoulder, not from the elbow, wrist, or fingers. Don't allow the arms to break at the wrist or for the fingers to float. Reach out with energy through the fingertips as if you are bobbing a ball underneath your hands.

Half Roll Up

Strengthen Stomach

Practise Flowing Movement and Control

Take care to work correctly in this exercise, using your deep abdominals rather than lurching the spine up or allowing other muscles to overwork.

1 Sit tall, then use your belly to curl your upper body over your legs, reaching the arms in line with the legs. Your nose reaches down towards your knees. Flex the feet away. Keep the belly lifted in and up. Imagine your spine lengthening like a spring.

Why? Flexing the feet ensures the legs are long and active, stretching the back of the thigh and providing a balance to the upper body as it moves.

2 Breathe in deeply as you start to roll your spine beneath you, controlling with your abdominals to release bone by bone towards the mat. Roll as far as you are able to control the movement, and hold it there for 3 breaths. Deeply engage the abdominals, and relax the shoulders and neck.

Remember Control is key. Make sure you go only as far as you are able to control the movement. Build up your strength slowly. Each time, go a little farther as your strength develops.

3 As you breathe out, deepen your scoop and squeeze the inner thighs and buttocks as you begin to roll back up and over the legs once more. Repeat 5 times. Each time, try to challenge yourself a little bit more to roll deeper, with control. Moving very slowly means you need to work the muscles harder because you can't rely on momentum.

Imagine Length is very important here. Imagine each bone of your spine reaching away from the one before it, lifting like bubbles as you move forwards.

Take care...

Don't hold your breath. Make sure you keep breathing. When you are holding the position, deepen your abdominals further with each out breath and check that the rest of your body is free from tension: jaw, neck, and shoulders.

Don't hunch your shoulders. Keep them soft and connected into the body as you curl.

Don't lift the feet. Stay heavy and grounded through the feet.

Mini Bridge

Strengthen Buttocks and Arms • **Practise** Concentration

This variation on the Shoulder Bridge (see pp.78–79) is great for building strength in your back and concentrating on your body. You use your body weight as resistance to build strength.

1 Align yourself centrally on your mat, legs lengthened on the floor with your feet flexed, arms relaxed by your sides, palms down. Breathe in to prepare and lengthen the spine.

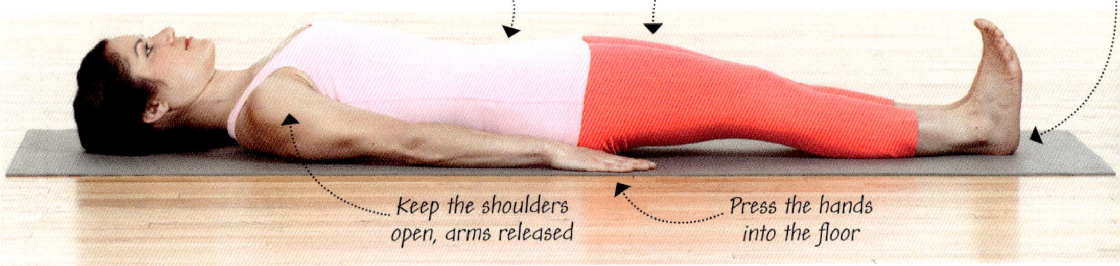

2 Breathe out, engage the powerhouse and press the hips up, lifting the buttocks off the mat. Feel the shoulders, arms, and heels pressing actively into the floor. Squeeze the legs strongly from the big-toe joints to the inner thighs. Hold for 5 breaths, not allowing the hips to drop. Slowly lower back down. Repeat 3 times.

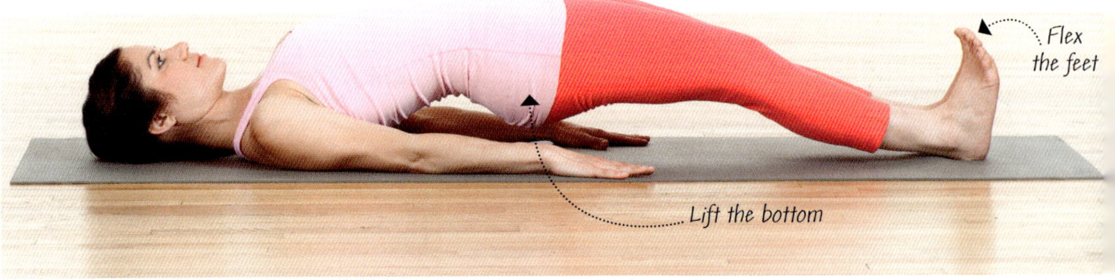

Letter T

Strengthen Upper back • **Practise** Flowing Movement

Great for your posture, this exercise strengthens the muscles between the shoulder blades and tones the arms and shoulders too. To add a challenge, hold hand weights in each hand.

1 Lie on your front, legs together and in parallel. Engage your powerhouse to peel the front of the body off the mat, reaching the arms out to the sides, in line with your shoulders. Keep your eyes focused down towards the mat and the neck long. Breathe in to prepare and lengthen the spine.

2 Breathe out to float the arms behind you and towards each other, reaching away with fingertips, lifting your chin and chest. Feel the shoulder blades gliding into the back. Breathe in to float back slowly to the start position. Repeat 5 times.

Rolling Like a Ball 2

Strengthen Stomach • **Practise** Breathing

Use your powerhouse to maintain a C-curve and move with flow and control. This is a playful exercise, bringing to mind the carefree movement of a child.

1 While sitting, create a C-curve with your spine. Fold the knees in towards your forehead, keeping them hip-width apart. Hold the ankles, feet together. Tip back off your sitting bones, float the feet off the ground, and look down towards your navel. Deepen the scoop of your belly, hold your legs in tight to create a ball shape. Maintain this position throughout.

Why? The deep abdominal scoop is needed to create a C-shape and support the spine in order to prevent unwanted movement.

2 Breathe in to roll back, maintaining the C-curve by using your abdominals. You should feel each vertebra rolling evenly. Make sure your position does not change as you are rolling back. Keep the eyes focused in towards your centre. Stay in a strong C-curve.

Imagine To help maintain the position, imagine an unbreakable magnetic connection between your heels and your bottom, and your nose and your belly.

3 Roll all the way back to the shoulder blades, no farther, sending your tailbone to the ceiling. Breathe out and roll back to the start position. Repeat up to 10 times, balancing momentarily between each roll. Keep your C-curve position throughout.

Help! If this feels very difficult, go back to your seated C-curve (see p.36) and really try to maintain this position as you roll. It takes time, but practice makes perfect!

Take care...

Don't roll your head back; keep it focused between the knees. If you look up, your back will straighten and you will end up stranded on the mat like a beetle on its back, unable to roll back up.

Try not to lose the C-curve. Don't allow the back to straighten when you reach the top of the roll. Keep the belly working when you balance at the end.

Your heels should not kick up to the ceiling. Keep the shins tightly drawn in towards you to avoid kicking the legs up. Maintain your ball shape throughout.

Keep the flow. This movement should be brisk and continuous. Ensure you breathe in to roll back, out to roll forwards, and keep the momentum going.

1 **2** 3

Single Leg Stretch 2

Strengthen Stomach • **Practise** Precision

This version of Single Leg Stretch 1 (see p.64) requires more focus as you pick up speed and coordinate your hand and leg movements. Work hard on maintaining a strong, stable torso.

1 Curl up, hugging your right knee into your chest. Put your right hand on your right ankle, and left hand across the knee. Reach your left leg away, in line with the body, and as low as you can take it without losing control of your spine. Breathe in to prepare.

2 Breathe out to switch legs and swap hand positions. Continue to alternate, breathing in to lengthen one leg and breathing out to return and lengthen the other. With each movement, maintain your deep belly scoop throughout.

Single Straight Leg Stretch

Strengthen Stomach • **Practise** Flowing Movement

Also known as "scissors", this exercise requires controlled, brisk movements that work your core and dynamically stretch the hamstrings.

1 Lie on your back, with the box square on the mat. Hug your knees to your chest and curl your forehead to your knees. Reach your right leg up to the ceiling and hold the ankle with both hands. Reach your left leg out in front of you. Turn the legs out in Pilates stance. Breathe out to pulse twice quickly with the right leg, stretching the hamstring as you draw the leg in towards your head.

Imagine Think of the pulse as a heartbeat, rhythmically pulling the leg in twice, then pressing away.

2 Breathe in to swap the leg positions, then pulse twice with the left leg while breathing out. Switch legs rapidly, keeping the torso absolutely still as you scissor the legs in and out. Repeat 8 times on each leg.

Careful! Keep the powerhouse working to ensure the body does not rock or bounce with the leg movement.

Double Leg Stretch 2

Strengthen Stomach • **Practise** Centring

This version of Double Leg Stretch requires more control and strength than stage 1 (see p.65). As you lengthen all four limbs away from the centre, you must maintain a stable spine and take care not to arch the back.

1 Lie flat, hugging the knees in towards your chest, taking the hands around the shins. Breathe out, use your abs and curl up, looking in towards your navel. Deepen your abdominal connection and feel the lower back releasing towards the mat.

Help! If your neck feels strained, do this exercise with your hands behind the head until you have the abdominal strength.

2 Breathe in and reach the arms behind you, in line with your ears, while you simultaneously press the legs away, squeezing the legs together in Pilates stance. Sink your abdominals into the spine as you reach the limbs away.

Imagine To maintain this position, imagine your spine is anchored, so there is no movement as you reach the limbs away.

3 Breathe out, open the arms out to the sides and down towards the hips, extending the fingertips forwards. Bend the knees in to return to the start position. Stay curled up, and repeat up to 6 times.

Careful! Precision is the key. Make sure you control the movement of the limbs and only take them within a safe range of movement for your spine. Build up your strength gradually.

Take care...

Don't let the head fall back as you reach the arms and legs away. Make sure you maintain your curl and keep the eyes focused downwards as the arms stretch back.

Don't let the ribcage move. Keep it locked in position as the arms move fluidly.

Avoid arching the lower back as the legs release forwards. Keep the belly strong to make sure the lower spine is heavy towards the mat. If necessary, keep the legs higher.

Don't let the arms carry the ribcage up. Stay strong in your centre as you reach the arms freely behind you.

Spine Stretch Forwards 2

Strengthen Stomach • **Practise** Breathing

A progression from stage 1 (see p.66), this version challenges your abdominals further by adding the weight of your arms to the movement. Focus on perfecting your C-curve.

1 Sit tall on your mat, with your legs in parallel, slightly wider than hip-width apart and heels pressing away. Float the arms above you, in line with the ears. Lift the belly in and up. Breathe in to prepare.

Imagine Your pelvis is anchored into the ground, and your spine is light, like a balloon lifting up away from the anchored sitting bones.

2 Breathe out, lift the spine up as you roll forwards, releasing the crown of the head towards your feet. Keep the arms in line with the ears and reach them over the feet. Deepen the abdominals. Keep the legs pressing away, activating the buttocks.

Imagine Picture someone pulling your waist back as you reach your fingertips forwards.

Careful! Don't let the front of your body collapse as you curl forwards. Lift even higher to resist the curl.

3 Breathe in and send the tailbone down to roll the spine back up sequentially. Float the arms up in line with the ears, shoulders relaxing into the back as you reach to the ceiling. Stay lifted through the abdominals and waist as you finish. Repeat 5 times.

Help! If you feel your shoulders hunching forwards, connect your shoulder blades into the back and lengthen the neck, releasing the crown of the head forwards.

Take care...

Don't hinge at the hips. Make sure your abdominals create the movement by moving with an active C-curve of the spine.

Your legs should not be floppy. Check the legs are in parallel, heels pressing out and back of the legs active, as you curl forwards and as you rebuild the spine.

Don't hunch your shoulders. Keep your neck long and feel your shoulder blades gliding into the back as you reach forwards.

Don't collapse the front of the body. Resist gravity with your abdominals: lift up as you bend forwards, as if someone has their hands around your waist from behind and is pulling your ribcage up.

Neck Roll

Strengthen Upper Back • **Practise** Control

An extension of the Swan Preparation (see p.69), this is a good stretch for the abdominals, using a lot of abdominal control to support the lower spine. When ready, you can move on to the Swan (see p.164).

1 Lie face down on the mat, legs connected. Keep the hands directly under the shoulders and elbows up towards the ceiling, hugging into your waist. Breathe in, lift your pelvic floor, and draw your belly in.

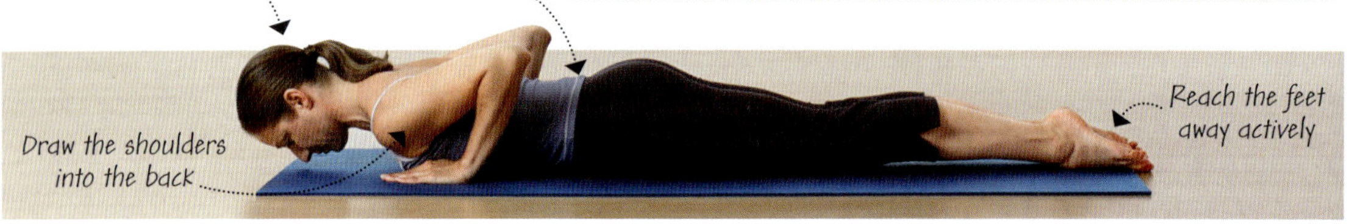

2 Breathe out, and roll the head and neck forwards and up. Feel an even pressure into the hands as the elbows come towards the floor. Keep the shoulders soft into the back.

3 Keep the belly scooped as you turn your gaze over one shoulder, to feel a gentle stretch in the neck. Keep your box square on the mat and avoid twisting the shoulders or ribs.

4 Circle the head down slowly to bring the chin towards the chest. Keep the torso lifted. Roll the neck across to the other side and look over that shoulder. Stay lengthened in the neck.

Careful! Maintain your powerhouse throughout to protect the lower back and to stop the belly dropping to the mat.

5 Bring your gaze back to the centre, and then repeat to the other side. Make sure you stay lifted and strong throughout. Repeat twice in each direction.

Help! If you feel your shoulders or lower back straining, bring your arms slightly in front of you to relieve the pressure. If you feel the lower back sinking and straining, lift the belly in more.

Magic Circle: Chest and Overhead

Strengthen Arms and Chest • **Practise** Control

This fabulous piece of equipment adds another dimension to your practice. Here, you will tone the arms and shoulders.

Chest Stand in the Pilates stance. Hold the Circle in line with your chest. Press into the pads, fingers long. Breathe in. Stand tall, breathe out to compress the Circle, activating the shoulders. Hold for 3 counts, then release slowly with control. Repeat 5 times.

Overhead Stay lengthened and relaxed in the spine as you work the arms. Float the Circle above the head, keeping the arms slightly in front of you. Breathe out to press the pads of the Circle. Hold for 3 counts, then slowly release. Repeat 5 times.

Magic Circle: Pumping

Strengthen Arms and Shoulders • **Practise** Centring

Here you will add movement, so you need to flow and avoid wobbling. Use your powerhouse to make sure the torso is strong and stable as you move the arms.

1 Stand in the Pilates stance. Hold the Circle out in front, at hip height. Keep your arms extended and elbows soft. Breathing naturally, pump the Circle 8 times as you raise it above your head. Keep the shoulders soft and down.

2 Pump 8 times to return to the start position. Repeat 3 times. The arms should float without affecting the position of the shoulders or spine. Keep the spine long and stable, eyes focused forwards, and legs squeezed together.

Magic Circle: Pliés

Strengthen Inner Thighs and Buttocks • **Practise** Control

A wonderful toner for the bottom and thighs, this balletic movement is great for your balance too. Avoid this exercise if you have weak knees.

1 Stand tall, with your hands on your hips. Keep the legs in the Pilates stance and bent, knees directly over the toes. Place the Circle between the fleshy part of your thighs, just above the knees. Your spine should be long and neutral.

2 From your powerhouse, squeeze the Circle to straighten the legs. Hold the Circle steady and lengthen the crown of the head to the ceiling. Bend your knees back to the starting position and repeat the exercise 3–5 times.

Magic Circle: Inner Thighs and Arms

Strengthen Inner Thighs and Arms • **Practise** Concentration

These seated exercises require focus on your alignment and posture. Engage your powerhouse throughout, keeping the waist narrow and lifted.

Inner thighs Place the Circle between your thighs, feet flat on the floor. Fold your arms in front, shoulders relaxed. Lengthen the spine. Breathe out, squeeze from the powerhouse, holding for 3 counts as you breathe in. Relax, breathing out. Repeat 3–5 times.

Arms Hold the Circle out in front. Keep the legs parallel, hip-width apart. Lift your heels, pressing down into the balls of the feet and the toes. Squeeze the Circle between your palms, activating the chest and arms. Keep the spine long and neutral. Repeat 3–5 times.

Neck Pull

Strengthen Stomach • **Practise** Control

This is a tough yet rewarding exercise. You will need strong abdominals, because holding the arms behind the head places more load on those muscles. Try it with your arms crossed in front instead and feel the difference.

1 Sit tall, with legs out in front, hip-width apart and in parallel. Press out through the heels. Take your hands behind your head, placing one hand on top of the other. Lift into your centre and lengthen the waist. Breathe in to hinge back from the hips.

Careful! If you feel this in the lower back as you hinge back, lift up your abdominals and engage the buttocks.

2 Hinge to the lowest point you can without arching the back. Then breathe out to begin to curl the tailbone underneath you, nod the chin to the chest, and curl your spine into a C-curve, with waist lifted and long. Try to perform this movement perfectly.

Imagine Think of your spine as a spring, stretching and lengthening.

3 Continue to move while breathing out, the belly constantly lifted as you roll your spine forwards, and send the nose over the knees. If you want to work harder, roll forwards to a full spine stretch (see pp.104–105) with hands behind the head. Re-stack the spine tall and strong. Repeat 5 times.

Imagine Think of the ribcage being lifted to the ceiling; resist the pull with your muscles.

Take care

Try not to curl or arch your spine. Challenge your strength to hinge back as far as you can without curling the spine or arching. Keep the legs heavy and reaching away.

Don't lift and bend the legs as you hinge back. Make sure you actively reach away through the feet and imagine someone is sitting on your legs to weigh them down.

Don't let the abdominals collapse as you reach forwards. Keep lifting continually throughout the exercise; never loosen the corset of muscles around the waist.

Don't hug your head with your elbows. Keep the elbows open and wide.

Side Kicks: Front 2

Strengthen Buttocks and Thighs • **Practise** Centring

Perform this series of Side Kick exercises on one side before moving to the other. This is more demanding than Side Kicks: Front 1 (see pp.72–73); you can't use your front arm for balance.

1 Lie on your left side, lined up with the back of the mat, shoulders and hips stacked. Take both hands behind your head. Press the head into the hands, with your neck lengthening and active. Hinge your hips forwards so the legs aim towards the front corner of the mat. The legs are in parallel. Breathe in; lift the top leg.

Take care...

Don't move the spine with the leg. Keep your powerhouse working hard. The leg should move independently from the spine, without taking the bottom with it.

Don't let your top shoulder drop forwards. Use all your strength to resist the pull forwards. Stay strong in your centre and open in the chest.

Don't let the leg bend, drop, or lift at the knee. Lengthen it from the thighbone and keep it absolutely level.

2 Breathe out to swing the leg forwards, pulsing it twice at the end of the swing. Keep the spine totally stable; resist the movement of bringing the tailbone under with the leg. Scoop the belly deeply throughout.

Help! Keep the swing small if your spine can't resist moving. Build it up until you can freely swing the leg without affecting the spine.

3 Breathe in to sweep the leg back, taking it as far as you can to open the hip. Make sure the upper body does not collapse. Repeat up to 10 times. You can alternate flexing and pointing the foot.

Side Kicks: Scissors

Strengthen Back and Thighs

Practise Flowing Movement

This allows freedom of movement in the legs, working the thigh and buttock muscles and warming up the whole body.

1 Lie on your side, hand behind your head. Lift the ribs. Rest the palm of your top hand on the mat in front of your body for support. Squeeze your legs in the Pilates stance. Breathe in, using your centre to lift and lengthen the legs to hip height.

2 Breathe out to scissor the legs, taking the bottom leg forwards first. Reach the legs equally behind and in front of you. Scissor the legs forwards and back 6 times, maintaining a stable spine. Think about freeing the thigh joint, allowing mobility and fluidity with a strong, stable spine.

Careful! Don't forget to breathe throughout.

Take care

Don't dip your waist into the mat. Resist the urge to slump the spine, stay strong and lifted in your abdominals.

Don't swing your back with the legs. Focus on your strong centre and control the movement.

Don't let your head dip forwards. Keep the front of your body open.

3 Moving dynamically and breathing naturally, swing the legs for 6 more kicks, as swiftly as you can while controlling the movement. Keep checking your centre is active.

Imagine The spine shouldn't move. Think of a thread linking the tailbone to the crown of the head and keeping your torso absolutely still.

Side Kicks: Circles

Strengthen Buttocks and Thighs • **Practise** Precision

The precision of this exercise will tone your buttocks and thighs like nothing else. Make sure you keep your alignment and powerhouse active.

1 Lie on your side, using your mat to guide your alignment, shoulders and hips stacked. Press your head into your hand; place the top hand in front. Bring the feet to the front of your mat, legs in Pilates stance. Lengthen the top leg to hip height, toes softly pointed.

Take care...

Don't let your upper body slump. Keep your powerhouse working and reach the neck active and long.

Don't just wiggle your toes. Make sure the circling movement is from the thighbone, as if you're turning a cocktail stick in a glass.

Don't allow the circles to be uneven, wobbly shapes. Keep the circles precise: really visualize them. This means your muscles will have to work harder.

2 Breathe naturally as you circle the upper leg, keeping it in front of the bottom leg. The circles should be small, as if you're tracing the inside of a jam jar. Circle the leg 10 times.

3 Lengthen the top leg back in line with the body, and circle 10 times again, behind the bottom leg. Keep the belly working to make sure the torso doesn't wobble as you circle from the thigh.

Side Kicks: Inner Thighs

Strengthen Inner Thighs • **Practise** Concentration

This exercise really targets the areas others can't reach – toning the inner thighs. You'll feel the burn if you concentrate on moving with perfect alignment and control.

1 Lie on your side, using the mat to guide your alignment, with shoulders and hips stacked. Press your head into your hand. Bend the top leg in and take hold of the ankle, placing the foot flat on the floor. Rotate the bottom leg so that the knee is facing down.

Tip Keep the bottom leg turned out like a key turning in a lock. This will focus the work on the inner thigh.

Hold the ankle of the top leg

Point the toes towards the bottom foot

Leg position

2 Connect to your powerhouse and lift the left leg up as high as you can, squeezing the inner thigh. Kick up swiftly and then slowly lower. Breathe naturally throughout. Kick 10 times.

Remember Concentrate on the inner thighs doing the work and try to soften other parts of your body.

Take care...

Try not to move the upper body as the thighbone lifts. Lengthen out through the neck and keep the upper body strong and stable.

Don't lift your leg too high. Take it as far as you can without slumping the waist. Keep the ribcage lifted.

Open Leg Rocker Preparation

Strengthen Stomach • **Practise** Centring

Practise this to prepare for Open Leg Rocker (see pp.156–157). It needs harmony of all Pilates principles: smooth coordination with the breath, flowing movements, a strong, stable centre, and control.

1 Sit tall, draw the legs in towards your chest, holding them around the ankles. Balance, tipping back off the sitting bones. Keep the spine long, eyes focused forwards, and lift through the crown of the head. Draw the belly in strongly and lengthen the neck, shoulders soft and down.

Tip Try to find a serene balance, without any tension anywhere in the body.

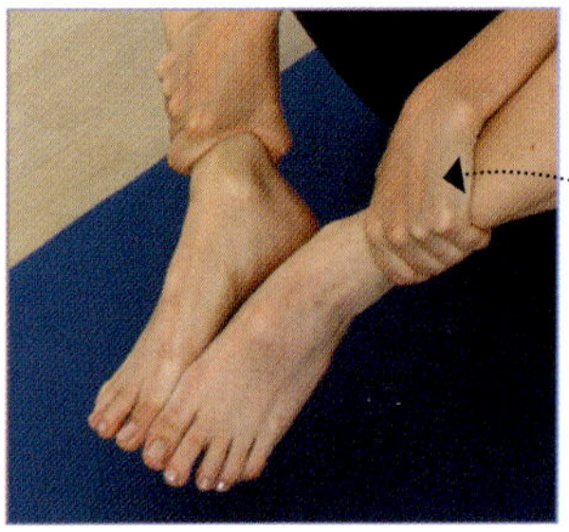

Position of hands

2 Breathe in as you lengthen both legs towards the ceiling, as straight as you can. Keep the upper body open. Breathe out and bend the knees, as for step 1. Repeat 2–3 times. Extend the legs once more and balance.

Careful! Try not to allow the tailbone to curl underneath you. Press the legs into the hands to help you to balance.

3 Breathe out and draw the legs together, squeezing your inner thighs, then open again. Stay long in the spine throughout and keep it supported. Bend the knees to return to the position shown in step 1. Repeat the sequence another 2–3 times.

Tip Concentrate on your balance, focusing on a point in front of you, and stay steady as you hold the legs strong.

Make it easier

Hold the legs around the knees instead, if you are finding it hard to maintain balance, Then softly bend the knees.

Take care...

Don't let the upper body collapse as you lengthen the legs. Use your powerhouse, abdominals, and the muscles between your shoulder blades to keep the body strong and open.

Teaser Preparation

Strengthen Stomach and Inner Thighs • **Practise** Control

This exercise builds up the strength for the Teaser (see pp.170–175), by breaking it down, precisely and slowly strengthening the deep abdominals and inner thighs.

1 Lie on your back, with feet flat on the floor. Float the arms above and behind you. Keep the ribcage heavy on the mat and abdominals flat.

Careful! Keep the ribcage heavy as you take the arms above you, to avoid the back arching.

2 Breathe out to float the arms above the head and forwards, nod the chin towards the chest and curl the spine off the mat. Scoop the belly in.

Imagine Think of your spine as a feather, being lifted lightly from the floor without strain.

3 Keep your C-curve until you find your tailbone, then open the chest and straighten the back. Breathe in to lengthen the spine. Breathe out and roll down slowly, bone by bone, to the start. Repeat 3 times.

Why? By moving on the out breath, the abdominal muscles can be more deeply recruited as you expel air from the lungs.

More of a challenge

To make it harder, when you reach the top, lengthen one leg away, squeezing the knees together and keeping the spine long. Hold this position for 1 or 2 breaths, making sure you don't curl the tail underneath you or collapse the chest. Float the foot down and repeat with the other leg. Then roll down as before and repeat 3 times.

Teaser with Twist

Strengthen Stomach • **Practise** Centring

This exercise is a very effective waist whittler. It demands a lot of strength from your waist. You'll need rock-solid abdominals and great core control for this.

1 Sit tall, with your legs connected. Reach your arms above the knees. Lengthen the right leg, keeping the knees squeezed together. Breathe in to lengthen the spine as you reach the leg away, to avoid collapsing, and scoop the belly.

Imagine Try to feel as if you are being lifted towards the ceiling.

2 Breathe out, deepen the abdominals, and curl the spine down, rolling bone by bone, to the shoulder blades. Breathe in. Keep your eyes focused forwards.

Remember Think about lift and length. Try to avoid your body collapsing and stay strong.

3 Breathe out and curl up, then twist the body across the extended leg. Return to centre as you breathe in. Repeat 3 times, twisting to each side.

Help! The abdominals will want to bunch as you twist. Keep scooping deeply to really connect to the powerhouse.

What not to do

Take care…

Don't twist from the shoulders, twist from the waist. Feel the twist deeply in the obliques, right under the ribcage.

Don't let the chest collapse. Keep the shoulders open and square as you move the torso. Keep thinking of your box.

Don't lower or bend the extended leg. Keep reaching out through this leg. Stay strong in the inner thighs and the powerhouse.

Swimming

Strengthen Upper Back and Buttocks
Practise Flowing Movement

A fast-moving exercise that tones the back and buttocks, and shows how Pilates strengthens the body by focusing on symmetrical movement. Concentrate on working each side evenly, with length.

1 Lie face down. Engage your centre deeply as you lengthen the arms and legs away and up. The arms are at shoulder height and the legs in Pilates stance.

Imagine Think about working under water: feel the resistance and the flow of the body against the water.

2 Extend the spine so your gaze is focused forwards. Reach your right arm and left leg away. Keep the belly strong.

Careful! Keep the lower spine long, hips open, and belly working throughout to protect the lower back.

3 Pick up the pace as you move the opposite arms and legs up and down in a swimming motion. Breathe in for 5 counts, then out for 5. Stay strong. Continue for up to 30 counts. Then relax back down.

Leg Swings: Front

Strengthen Core and Buttocks • **Practise** Precision

This exercise teaches you to move freely, almost like you did when you were a child. It pumps the heart rate, challenges your balance, and checks your posture.

1 Stand tall, squeezing the legs in Pilates stance, with your arms crossed in front. Connect to your powerhouse, with shoulders relaxed and neck long. Deeply draw the abdominals in and up towards the spine.

2 Breathe out and swing the right knee in towards your chest. Keep the spine long, avoid tucking in the pelvis. Place the foot down swiftly as you breathe in. Switch legs. Repeat, to do 10 on each side.

Leg Swings: Side

Strengthen Hips • **Practise** Control

This exercise is wonderful if you suffer from tight hips. Strong core and balance is needed to ensure no movement ricochets through the rest of the body.

1 Stand tall in the Pilates stance. Keep the arms out at shoulder height, palms facing downwards. Lengthen your neck. Connect to your powerhouse and soften the shoulders. Breathe in to prepare.

Tip Keep the torso long and stable. Make sure the shoulders stay level. It helps to practise this in front of a mirror.

2 As you breathe out, kick your right knee up and out to the side, towards the elbow. Lower the leg. Alternate the legs, increasing the energy of the movement each time. Maintain a strong and stable centre.

Imagine Feel the crown of your head being pulled up towards the ceiling as you swing the leg.

15-Minute Sequence

1 Ten by Ten
pp.92–93

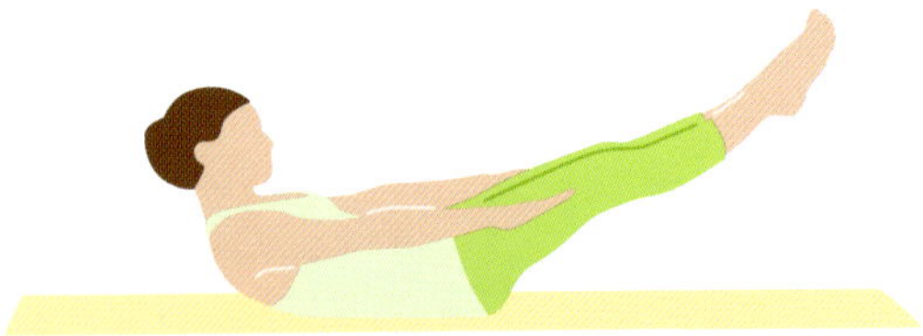

2 Half Roll Up
pp.94–95

5 Single Leg Stretch 2
p.100

6 Double Leg Stretch 2
pp.102–103

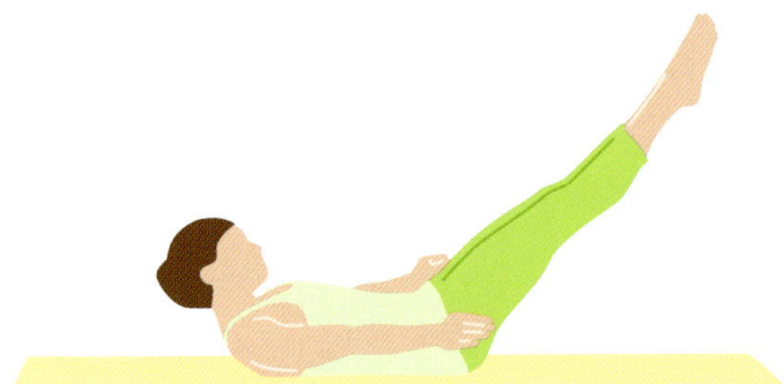

9 Side Kicks: Scissors
pp.116–117

10 Teaser Preparation
pp.124–125

3 Rolling Like a Ball 2
pp.98–99

4 Mini Bridge
p.96

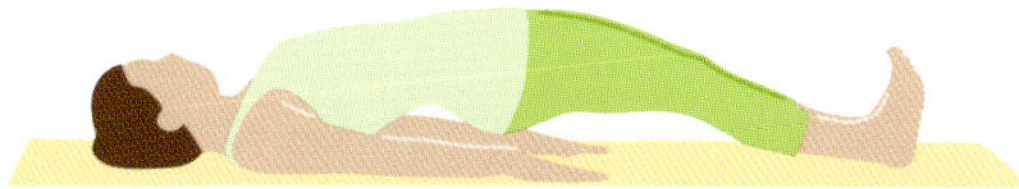

7 Neck Roll
pp.106–107

8 Side Kicks: Front 2
pp.114–115

11 Swimming
pp.128–129

12 Leg Swings: Front
p.130

30-Minute Sequence

1 **Ten by Ten**
pp.92–9

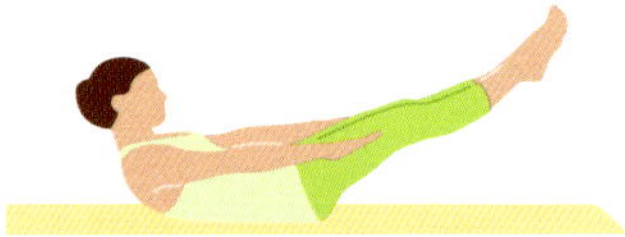

2 **Half Roll Up**
pp.94–95

3 **Rolling Like a Ball 2**
pp.98–99

7 **Mini Bridge**
p.96

8 **Single Leg Stretch 2**
p.100

9 **Double Leg Stretch 2**
pp.102–103

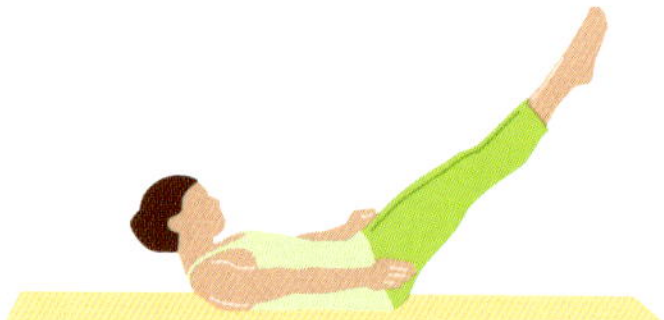

13 **Neck Roll**
pp.106–107

14 **Spine Stretch Forwards 2**
pp.104–105

15 **Neck Pull**
pp.112–113

19
Magic Circle: Pliés
p.110

4 **Side Kicks: Front 2**
pp.114–115

5 **Side Kicks: Scissors**
pp.116–117

6 **Side Kicks: Circles**
pp.118–119

10 **Open Leg Rocker Preparation**
pp.122–123

11 **Teaser Preparation**
pp.124–125

12 **Swimming**
pp.128–129

16 **Leg Swings: Front**
p.130

17 **Leg Swings: Side**
p.131

18 **Magic Circle: Inner Thighs and Arms**
p.111

45-Minute Sequence

1 Ten by Ten
pp.92–93

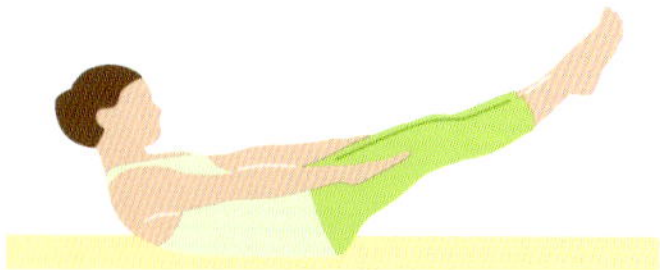

2 Half Roll Up
pp.94–95

3 Rolling Like a Ball 2
pp.98–99

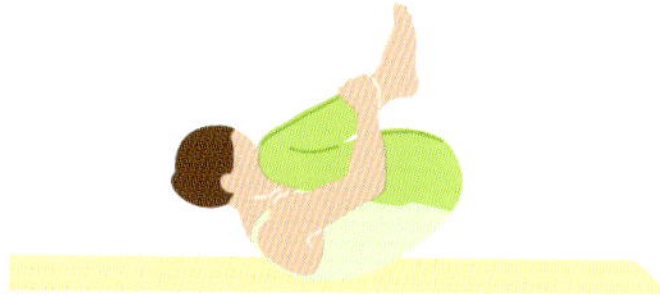

7 Mini Bridge
p.96

8 Single Leg Stretch 2
p.100

9 Single Straight Leg Stretch
p.101

13 Double Leg Stretch 2
pp.102–103

14 Neck Roll
pp.106–107

15 Spine Stretch Forwards 2
pp.104–105

19 Neck Pull
pp.112–113

20 Side Kicks: Front 2
pp.114–115

21 Side Kicks: Scissors
pp.116–117

4 Side Kicks: Circles
pp.118–119

5 Side Kicks: Inner Thighs
pp.120–121

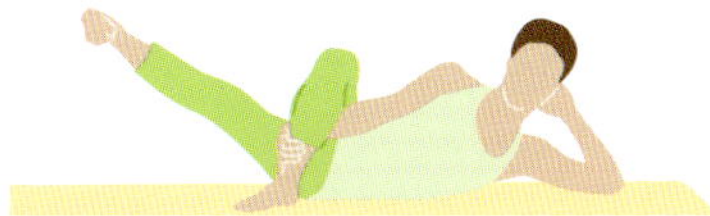

6 Open Leg Rocker Preparation
pp.122–123

10 Teaser Preparation
pp.124–125

11 Letter T
p.97

12 Swimming
pp.128–129

16 Leg Swings: Front
p.130

17 Leg Swings: Side
p.131

18 Magic Circle: Chest and Overhead
p.108

22 Magic Circle: Pumping
p.109

23 Magic Circle: Inner Thighs and Arms
p.111

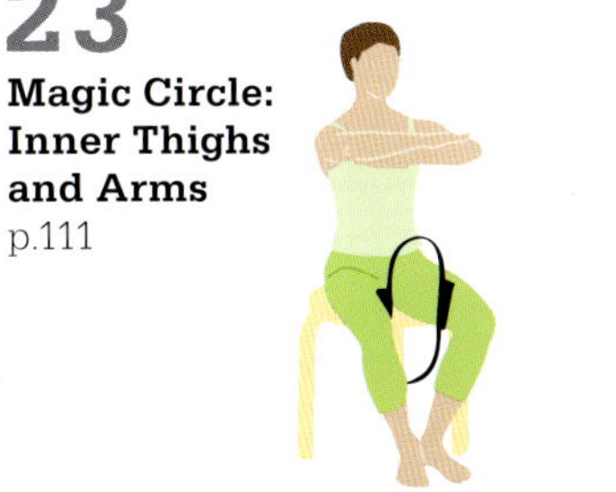

24 Magic Circle: Pliés
p.110

Assess your progress

How did you progress over the last six weeks? Go back and check your baselines (see pp.90–91). How do you feel compared to the first time you performed the exercises? Did you notice an improvement? If so, well done! Keep at it!

Common problems

Have you made less progress than you had hoped? Don't be discouraged. Pilates at this stage presents an even greater challenge: the more you understand, the more you will realize there is to understand. You should by now be concentrating on all the various techniques and principles while you exercise, so you will have more body awareness and will be more aware of any weaknesses. This is a good thing, so don't worry or allow your enthusiasm to flag. Remember Pilates is all about the detail – if you are struggling, always revisit the basics and the principles, and the answers may be found there. Here are some common problems that you might face at this stage.

"It's hard to coordinate my breathing to the movement."

As long as you're breathing rather than holding your breath, you're halfway there. The breathing pattern is one of the most common things that people struggle with, so you're not alone. At this stage, the exercises become more dynamic and the need for controlled, coordinated breathing is greater. Memorize the exercise's breathing pattern: then, you will know exactly what you should be doing and won't lose focus during the exercise. Concentrate solely on breathing for a few workouts: you will begin to find it makes sense in your body and with the movement. Above all, never hold your breath as you move, because it will make you tense.

"I find the side-lying exercises really difficult on one side."

This is very common: Pilates will highlight any imbalances that we have in the muscles and skeleton. Often, we favour one side of the body more than the other in daily movement, which causes it to become stronger. If you find the exercises on one side significantly harder and your body less stable, don't give up. Perform more repetitions on this side to try to strengthen it and balance the body.

"I simply can't do a particular exercise."

Keep practising; it will come. Break the exercise down and practise each section individually to work out which part is causing you trouble. Repeat this movement over and over, to train both your body and mind. Being determined will reap rewards. If a particular exercise is causing you pain or aggravating a part of the body, however, it is probably best to avoid the exercise, or substitute another one for it. For example, if your lower back is aggravated by a rolling exercise, omit it or replace it with one from the first chapter (see pp.26–87) until you feel stronger and more controlled, and able to tackle it again.

Assess your achievement

Didn't achieve your goals? Don't lose your inspiration as you move on to the final section of the book (see pp.140–185). Celebrate every achievement as you practise, for example being able to roll your spine smoothly into a C-curve, or to straighten your leg slightly farther, than before. Small achievements build up – soon you'll be setting yourself new goals.

Challenging exercises

Here is a plan to help you during your workouts over the next six weeks. At the end of the six weeks, look back over these goals and assess how you have progressed.

Goal: Control

Teaser with Twist (see pp.126–127)

Goal: Centring

Double Leg Stretch 2 (see pp.102–103)

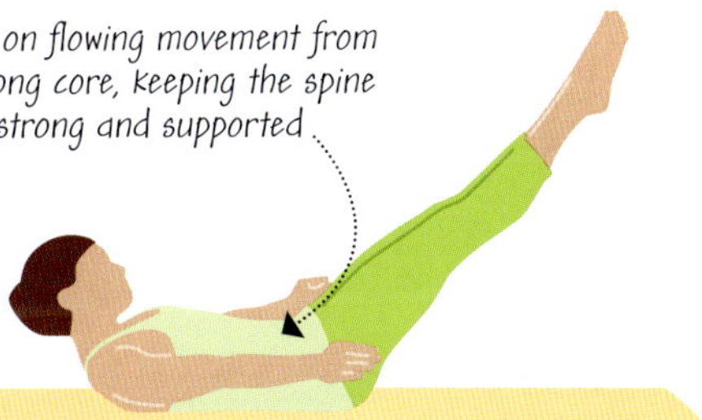

Goal: Flexibility

Single Straight Leg Stretch (see p.101)

Goal: Strength

Ten by Ten (see pp.92–93),
Half Roll Up (see pp.94–95),
Teaser Preparation (see pp.124–125)

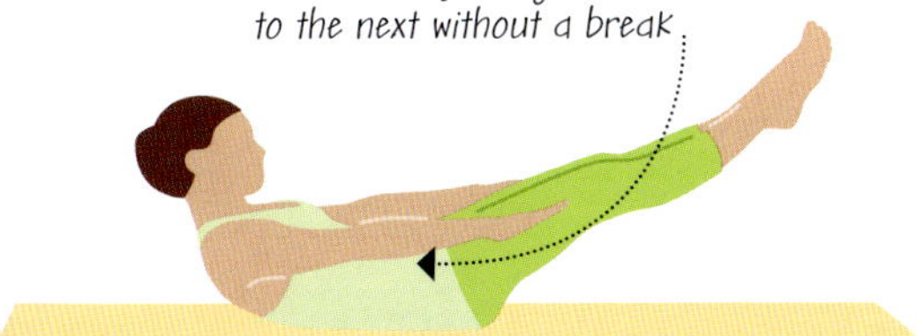

Goal: Flowing Movement

Swimming (see pp.128–129)

3

Take It Further

The exercises in this chapter require you to have mastered all of the earlier exercises as well as to understand and be able to put in to practice the fundamental principles of Pilates. Perform each of these final, more demanding exercises precisely, fluidly, and purposefully, only moving on to the sequences once you are fully confident with your ability to perform each individual exercise. Once you have completed the course in this book, you should be well-equipped to continue practising Pilates, and will reap the benefits of a strong, supple, and balanced body.

Plan Your Programme

We're nearly at the end of the programme! You should be really seeing the results by now, with sculpted limbs, a supple spine, and a honed midriff, not to mention feeling brighter and clearer as you breathe more easily and stand taller.

Planning the next step

I hope your progress so far has inspired you to continue with just as much enthusiasm as you possessed at the start. Now we want to take the next challenge into the more advanced Pilates exercises on the mat, working our bodies even harder. Keep focusing on the detail and you will find that these dynamic exercises offer an amazing sense of achievement for your body. We will continue to use broadly the same goals as for the first two stages of the programme, so that we have a good idea of how far we have come when we reach the end.

Build On It Exercise Programme

Use this programme to set yourself goals and assess your progress over the next six weeks. Summaries of the sequences are on pp.178–183. Each week, when you workout, follow the sequences in this programme for the first few times. Then you could mix exercises in from the rest of the section – but take care to substitute any with an exercise that trains the same area of the body, so your workout is balanced. Remember to act as your own coach and perform every movement to the best of your ability.

Week 1: Focus on Alignment

Baseline: The original photographs you took at the start of the Start Simple Exercise Programme (see pp.28–29).

- **Day 1:** 30-minute sequence, check centring, control
- **Day 2:** 15-minute sequence, check lengthening, coordination
- **Day 3:** 45-minute sequence, check precision, flowing movement
- **Day 4:** 30-minute sequence, check stability, breathing.

Goal: take new photos after six weeks to see how much closer you are to your ideal alignment.

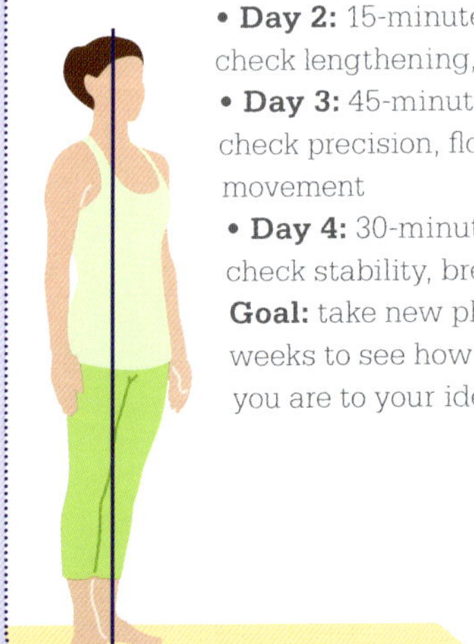

Week 2: Focus on Control

Baseline: perform the Corkscrew (see pp.160–161). Are you moving smoothly through the hips, or stiffly and jerkily? Can you hold the legs together and connect to your powerhouse throughout? Are the legs moving in a circle or more of a square?

- **Day 1**: 45-minute sequence, check centring, alignment
- **Day 2**: 30-minute sequence, check concentration, precision, scoop
- **Day 3:** 45-minute sequence, check precision, breathing, Pilates box
- **Day 4:** 15-minute sequence, check flowing movement, stability.

Goal: do the exercise with control, precision, and fluidity, remembering powerhouse, scooping, and lengthening.

Week 3: Focus on Centring

Baseline: perform Scissors (see pp.168–169). Is the back arched? Is the spine still and supported as you move the legs?

- **Day 1:** 30-minute sequence, check box, alignment, flowing movement
- **Day 2:** 30-minute sequence, check stability, precision, lengthening
- **Day 3:** 45-minute sequence, check precision, control, breathing
- **Day 4:** 30-minute sequence, check control, alignment.

Goal: no unwanted movement of the spine as you lengthen the limbs away, smoothly and in control.

Week 4: Focus on Flexibility

Baseline: perform Open Leg Rocker (see pp.156–157). Are you able to keep both legs straight up to the ceiling? Does your spine roll evenly on the floor?

- **Day 1:** 30-minute sequence, check precision, control, alignment
- **Day 2:** 30-minute sequence, check breathing, scoop, stability
- **Day 3:** 45-minute sequence, check scoop, powerhouse, coordination
- **Day 4:** 15-minute sequence, check control, concentration.

Goal: keep the legs straight and lengthened, and roll the spine through each vertebra evenly.

Week 5: Focus on Strength

Baseline: try performing Teaser 1, Teaser 2, and Teaser 3 (see pp.170–175) without a break. On a scale of 1 to 10, how hard was each exercise and the sequence?

- **Day 1:** 45-minute sequence, check centring, control, coordination
- **Day 2:** 30-minute sequence, check scoop, alignment, concentration
- **Day 3:** 15-minute sequence, check alignment, coordination, flowing movement
- **Day 4:** 45-minute sequence, check control, precision, powerhouse.

Goal: when you do the sequence again, it should feel easier.

Week 6: Focus on Flowing Movement

Baseline: perform Rocking (see pp.176–177). Does the movement feel fluid and controlled or jerky and broken? Can you rock smoothly without stopping and starting?

- **Day 1:** 30-minute sequence, check centring, breathing, coordination
- **Day 2:** 45-minute sequence, check stability, control, Pilates box
- **Day 3:** 15-minute sequence, check alignment, lengthening, coordination
- **Day 4:** 45-minute sequence, check precision, centring, breathing.

Goal: make the movement smoother as you engage your powerhouse to begin rocking, without any wobbling or stopping.

Check your new baseline for each area of the body before you begin this exercise programme and make a note of how it feels to do each movement. Then, at the end of the six weeks, assess yourself, according to the goals given here, to see how far you have gone towards achieving your targets. Enjoy the next six weeks!

The Hundred

Strengthen Stomach • **Practise** Breathing

Joe Pilates's original "classic" version of The Hundred requires deep abdominal strength, control, and precision. It warms up the body and fires up the powerhouse.

1 Lie on your mat, shoulders open, arms relaxed by your sides, and your legs reaching away, connected in the Pilates stance. Lift into your powerhouse, squeeze the legs, and breathe in to prepare.

Take care...

Don't tilt your head back. Keep your neck long and eyes forwards. Use your belly to curl up more, rather than allowing the neck to drop back.

Don't let your arms become floppy. Your arms should pump from the shoulder joint freely, pressing out through the palms.

2 Breathe out, scoop your belly, and curl the head and shoulders off the mat, reaching your arms forwards with energy. Keep the neck long and shoulders away from your ears. Simultaneously, lift your legs away, keeping them as close to the floor as you can control.

Careful! If you feel a strain in the neck or lower back, bring the legs slightly higher and deepen your abdominal connection.

3 Breathe in and pump the arms dynamically for a count of 5. Breathe out and pump for another count of 5. Give a long, even exhalation as you pump, and not a staccato breath. Suspend the head and legs easily in space as you pump smoothly. Repeat this pattern until you reach 100 pumps. Pause to lengthen the body, then release down with control.

Imagine Think of lightness. It should look effortless, not strained.

Roll Over

Strengthen Stomach, Thighs, Buttocks, and Arms
Practise Concentration

A massage for the spine, this exercise works the abdominals to peel the spine smoothly from the mat. You need control and a strong core to prevent momentum from carrying the legs over.

1 Lie on your mat. Engage your centre. Float your legs into the chest, then extend them up to the ceiling. Rotate your legs into the Pilates stance, engaging the buttock and thigh muscles.

Remember Squeeze the legs together from the inner thighs to the heels. Feel the buttocks wrapping around, connecting the legs tightly.

2 Breathe out, curl the spine bone by bone to lift the hips, sending the legs over the head, parallel with the floor. Work the arms to support your body weight.

Why? The legs are active, so you are aware of the whole body contributing to the dynamics of the movement.

3 Breathe in and flex the feet. Breathe out and lower down with control, bone by bone. Keep the legs straight and reaching away.

Imagine Think of having spines on your back like those on a dinosaur's back. Each of these must lock into the floor individually as your torso rolls down.

4 When you reach your tailbone, lengthen your legs towards the floor, with the belly strong and feet flexed. Close your legs into the Pilates stance, then use the strength of your belly to pick them up and roll over again. Repeat 5 times.

Careful! The legs tend to bend and become limp. Keep them active, lifted, and strong.

Climb a Tree

Strengthen Stomach • **Practise** Precision

This exercise clearly highlights any imbalances you have in your body. It requires great control and strength – with one leg in the air there is no way you can cheat!

1 Sit tall, left leg reaching away and right leg bent in towards you. Lengthen the right leg towards the ceiling, then bend it again. Repeat 3 times.

Remember Draw the belly in tight, waist long and chest open.

2 On the third reach, walk your hands up the leg to take hold of the ankle. Keep strong and lifted in the waist.

Tip Lift the body higher as if you are opening your chest towards your foot.

3 Breathe in. Lengthen the right leg to the ceiling as you curl the spine down, walking your hands down your leg. Go as far as your shoulder blades, keeping the eyes focused towards the knee.

Careful! Keep the movement slow. Don't let your body drop.

4 Breathe out and climb back up the leg with your hands. Try to straighten the leg as much as you can. Repeat twice; switch legs.

Help! If one side feels more difficult, use your abs to control it.

Footwork 1

Strengthen Thighs and Buttocks • **Practise** Concentration

This standing exercise works your muscles against gravity in a slightly unusual way. You need balance and focus to perform this correctly. Toned buttocks and thighs will be your reward!

1 Stand tall, in the Pilates stance. Release your shoulders into your back and lengthen the waist. Lift into your centre. Place the hands behind the head, keeping the elbows wide.

Remember Keep lifting through the crown of the head throughout.

2 Breathe in, bend the knees and lower the tailbone directly to the floor. The heels rise. At the bottom, press the heels down and rise back to standing. Repeat 6 times, breathing in to lower and breathing out to lift.

Careful! If you have knee problems, avoid this exercise.

Footwork 2

Strengthen Buttocks • **Practise** Precision

This is a simple exercise, but it requires control and precision. It will give great toning results if performed correctly. Think about your alignment and strong core throughout.

1 Stand tall, with the legs hip-width apart and in parallel. Keep the arms crossed in front of your chest and shoulders released and away from the ears. Draw the belly in towards the spine.

Remember Think about your box. Keep it long and square.

2 Bend your knees as low as you can while keeping your balance. Press yourself up, using your centre. Repeat 6 times. Breathe in to lower and breathe out to rise back up.

Imagine As you bend, think of your core like a dimmer switch, turning up its engagement to support the movement.

Double Straight Leg Stretch

Strengthen Stomach • **Practise** Control

This exercise hones the mid-section of the body well, tautening the waist and working on the six-pack. It also develops your strength and stamina.

1 Lie centrally on the mat, with legs in towards the chest. Keep the thighs soft and relaxed in their sockets. Take your hands behind your head, elbows wide and open, and breathe in to lengthen the spine.

2 Breathe out and curl the upper body off the mat, extending the legs towards the ceiling and squeezing them together in the Pilates stance. Engage the buttocks and thighs and softly point the feet. Look in towards your navel and scoop the belly.

Help! If this is tough on your thighs and you feel them gripping, bend the knees slightly.

3 Breathe in and lower the legs down towards the mat, only as far as you can control the movement. Breathe out and draw them back slowly, wrapping the buttock muscles around. Keep your upper body strong and still. Repeat 8 times.

Tip Focus on your centre, keeping the core strong as you lengthen the legs away.

Criss-cross

Strengthen Stomach and Waist • **Practise** Flowing Movement

This exercise is a waist cincher like no other. Focus on moving precisely, with flow. When you start to tire towards the end, keep moving with control and you will see dramatic results.

1 Start by doing the Double Straight Leg Stretch (see pp.152–53). Keep your hands behind your head and fold the knees in. Breathe in and curl up, press one leg away, and twist the spine towards the bent leg. Keep the elbows wide and the waist long. Pause.

2 Breathe out, switch legs, and rotate to the opposite knee. Keep the abdominals sinking towards the spine. Repeat 6 times on each side; as you twist from side to side, stay curled up. Then relax down.

Spine Stretch Forwards 3

Strengthen Upper Back and Stomach • **Practise** Breathing

This exercise combines Spine Stretch Forwards 1 (see p.66) and 2 (see pp.104–105), and involves moving through the spine with control, using the breath, and working the abs to stretch the spine.

1 Sit tall with the legs hip-width apart and in parallel, with the belly lifted in and up. Reach the arms in line with the legs, palms down and shoulders relaxed into the back. Breathe in to prepare.

2 Breathe out and roll the spine forwards in a C-curve, reaching the arms above and parallel to the legs. Breathe in to deepen the stretch. Breathe out to roll back up, bone by bone, growing taller as you re-stack.

Open Leg Rocker

Strengthen Stomach • **Practise** Control

Rhythm, balance, flexibility, core strength, and control are all required here. The rolling should appear smooth and effortless, but underneath there needs to be strict control and precision.

1 Sit on your mat with room to roll back. Float the legs to the ceiling, just wider than the shoulders, holding on around the ankles. Open your chest and connect your shoulders into your back. Connect deeply to your centre. Breathe in to prepare.

Imagine Think of your body as a perfect "V" shape.

2 Breathe out and, maintaining the same position, curl your tailbone under and allow yourself to rock back as far as your shoulder blades. Nod the chin to the chest and look at your centre.

Remember Keep the "V" shape as you rock back. Reach the thighbones away from your centre.

3 Breathe in, and pause at the bottom of the movement. Then breathe out and roll back up, activating the backs of the thighs. Balance at the top, with the chest open. Repeat up to 8 times. To finish, float your feet down.

Imagine Think of your spine as a wheel rolling on a track, rolling back and forth along exactly the same section evenly.

Take care...

Avoid tipping the head back. Let the movement come from the tilting of the hips, and then smoothly roll onto the spine. The head stays aligned at the end of the spine.

Don't hunch the shoulders. Doing this drags the body towards the legs. Keep the arms long and light, the shoulders connected down and back. The limbs stay exactly in position as the spine rocks the body.

Seal

Strengthen Back and Stomach • **Practise** Concentration

This exercise evokes the playful movement of childhood, while also toning the abdominals and massaging the spine. It is a great challenge for your core strength, balance, and coordination.

1 Sit tall on your mat. Thread your hands through your legs to take hold of the outsides of your ankles. Tilt your hips to lift your feet from the mat. Balance momentarily, scooping in your belly. Clap the insides of the feet together 3 times, imitating a seal. Lengthen the spine and draw in the belly.

Help! Practise this without the foot claps at first if it is too hard to coordinate the movement.

2 Breathe in and roll back smoothly, as far as the shoulder blades. Keep your chin tucked into your chest to make sure your head doesn't roll back. The tailbone reaches up towards the ceiling. Pause here momentarily and clap the feet 3 times once more.

3 Breathe out and deepen your powerhouse connection to roll back to the start position. Clap the feet as you balance, then roll back again smoothly. Repeat up to 10 times, breathing in to roll back and out to roll forwards. The movement is swift and fluid.

Tip Use your breath. The forceful exhalation helps you to connect to the abdominals and to muster the power to roll forwards with control.

Take care...

Don't drop your head back when initiating the roll. The head should nod towards the chest throughout the movement, keeping the neck long.

Don't straighten the back at the top of the movement. Keep the C-curve active throughout; you should feel as if you could roll continuously.

Corkscrew

Strengthen Stomach, Inner Thighs, and Buttocks
Practise Centring

Corkscrew requires strong control and a deep connection to your powerhouse. You need to move smoothly with no tension or strain as the abdominals take the weight of the legs.

1 Lie flat on the mat, legs stretched directly up above your hips. Imagine a clock face above you, with your legs pointing straight up to twelve o'clock. Soften the knees if you feel the thighs are gripping.

2 Breathe in and squeeze the legs together as you tilt the pelvis to rock across to your right and bring the legs to three o'clock. Keep the torso heavy. Move only the legs – the hips and ribs should not lift.

Make it easier

Place your hands on the mat to brace the lower back and press the elbows down to the mat. Follow the exercise. If you still have back pain while doing this exercise, stop.

Take care...

Make sure you keep your legs and feet glued together throughout. Feel the movement coming from the tops of the thighbones and pelvis.

Don't rock the shoulders or ribs. To isolate the movement in the hips, connect to your centre and concentrate on controlling the movement.

3 Circle the legs forwards and down to six o'clock, lowering them as they go. Keep the abdominals strongly scooped as you release the legs forwards. Feel the lower back supported by the abdominals.

4 Circle the legs across and up to nine o'clock, at your left. Breathe out to complete the circle and take the legs back to twelve o'clock. Repeat the whole circle, but in the opposite direction. Then repeat 2–3 sets.

Saw

Strengthen Waist and Back • **Practise** Breathing

Joe Pilates wanted us to "wring all the air out of the lungs" as you would wring water from a wet cloth. Here, bending the spine on the out breath facilitates this sensation.

1 Sit tall, the legs about shoulder-width apart, feet flexed. Float your arms out to the side, just within your peripheral vision, palms facing down, fingers long. Connect to your centre, lift the waist, and pull in the abdominals.

Tip Your spine is lifting and lengthening up and away from your pelvis. Your legs are long and active.

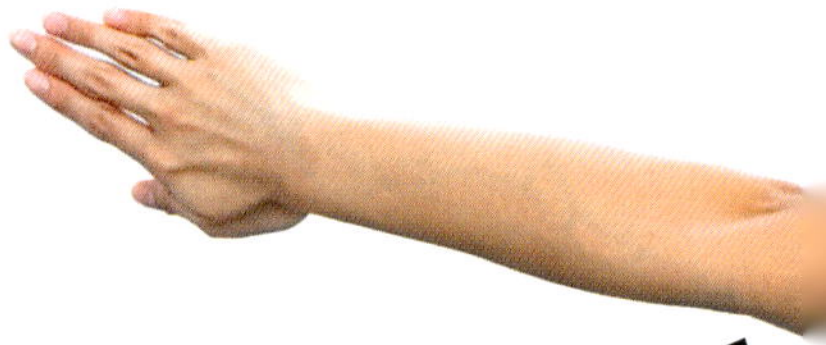

Take care...

Your legs shouldn't move with the twist. The twist should come from the ribs, not from the hips, so the pelvis should remain square. Check that your feet aren't moving as you twist, and keep the sitting bones bolted into the floor.

Don't allow the knees to roll in. Keep the feet and knees parallel with the ceiling to make sure you are in good alignment.

2 Breathe in as you twist to the right, imagining the spine growing taller as you twist. Keep the left hip anchored and square. Press out through the heels.

Imagine Think of your ribcage as a ball twisting around a pole connected to the ceiling. Grow taller as you twist.

3 Breathe out and curl the spine forwards, reaching the left hand to the outside of the right foot. Curl deeper. Breathe in to re-stack to your centre, then twist to the left. Repeat 3 times on either side.

Why? Breathing out while curling forwards softens the ribcage and facilitates the movement. Your belly lifts and the air is squeezed out of the lungs as you pulse farther forwards.

Swan

Strengthen Spine, Stomach, Arms, and Legs
Practise Flow, Breath, Control, and Precision

It is a challenge to perform this exercise correctly. Build up your strength with Swan Preparation (see p.69). Move your body as one connected unit, with strength and flow.

1 Lie face down on your mat. Squeeze your feet together, in parallel. Extend the spine, lifting the chest. Reach the arms out in front, pulling the shoulder blades down and into the back to connect. Draw the belly in to support the spine.

Tip Relax and lengthen the neck, keep the chest lifted.

2 Breathing naturally, begin to rock on your pelvis, initiating a small forwards and backwards movement, like a boat rocking on water. Use the powerhouse connection to increase the rocking.

Remember The momentum comes from your powerhouse, not from reaching with the arms or kicking the legs.

3 As the rocking increases, reach the legs up to the ceiling to increase the downwards momentum. Drive the chest up high to send the legs downwards. Repeat up to 10 times. Then counterstretch by rounding your back, bending your knees, lifting your bottom and sitting on your heels. Fold yourself into the Child's Pose (see p.17), with arms releasing forwards and chest towards your thighs. Relax the forehead downwards and allow the spine to release.

Tip Focus on keeping length in the body: reach the fingertips away from the toes and allow this extension to help you find the strength for the movement.

Take care...

Try not to break the line of the body. Keep the body connected from your toes right to the crown of the head – your centre should support the spine completely.

Don't bend your arm or legs. Reach with the limbs straight and dynamically away from your centre.

Make it easier

Double Leg Kick

Strengthen Upper Back and Back of Thighs
Practise Concentration

This exercise opens the chest, mobilizing the upper back and working the hamstrings. Concentrate on the muscles you should be feeling, to ensure they are working effectively.

1 Lie face down, turn your head to the right and rest on your cheek. Clasp your hands behind your back, elbows out to the sides. Relax the body into the mat, and draw in the belly. Relax and lengthen the spine.

2 Breathe in and kick the heels in towards the buttocks swiftly for 3 pulses. Support the lower back by releasing your hips and pelvis heavily into the mat as you kick the legs in – try not to arch. The spine remains still and stable – make sure your belly is scooped deeply.

Take care...

Don't let the hips rise as the legs kick. Keep the front of the pelvis heavy into the mat throughout the movement.

The elbows should not be too high. Keep the elbows low and out to the side.

3 Breathe out. Simultaneously reach the hands towards your buttocks as you lift straight legs. Stretch the arms back to lift the upper body. Pause here for a moment, then lower the body with control and turn the other cheek to the floor. Clasp the hands up the back and release the elbows to the sides. Repeat 3 times, alternating sides. Rest your bottom back onto your heels into the Child's Pose (see p.17) once you finish.

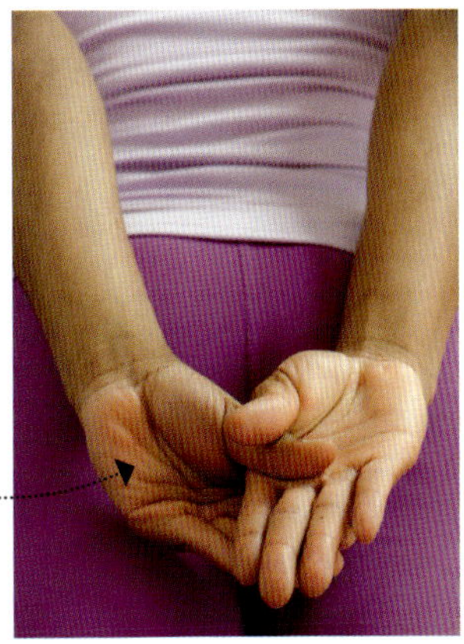

Hand position

Scissors

Strengthen Buttocks, Stomach, and Back • **Practise** Precision

This is an incredibly demanding exercise. Protect your shoulders and neck by maintaining a strong centre throughout and working with length and control.

1 Lie flat on your back with your legs extended above your hips and connected in Pilates stance. Place your arms by your sides and press them into the mat. Keep the palms down, fingertips actively pressing into the ground. Connect deeply to your powerhouse, with waist long, belly scooped.

2 Scoop your belly and lift the hips, raising your legs straight up to the ceiling, making sure they don't tip towards you. Take your hands behind your back for support, with elbows flat on the floor.

3 Allow the hips to lower slightly into the hands. Pause for a moment to draw in more deeply to your centre and feel balanced. Lengthen your box, scoop the belly, and feel the arms supporting your weight.

Careful! If you feel dizzy at any point, stop immediately.

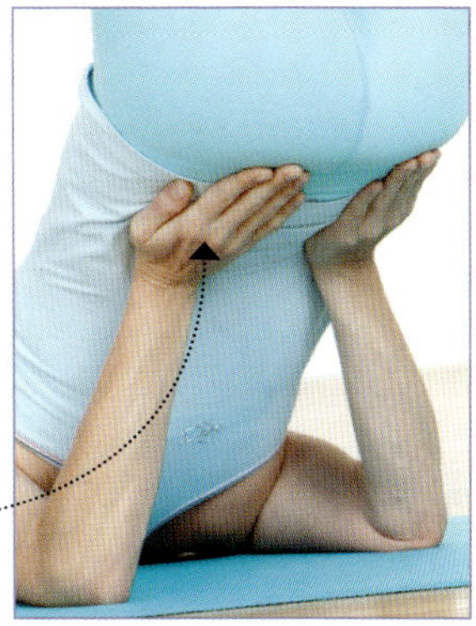

Hand position

4 Breathe in to scissor your legs. Breathe out and reverse. When familiar with the scissor movement, finish with a double pulse of the leg. Alternate for 5 sets. Release the hips back down slowly to finish.

Imagine Think of pressing your legs against resistance, as if stretching toffee between the legs.

Teaser 1

Strengthen Stomach • **Practise** Control

This exercise concentrates on the abdominals – its pure focus means there's no way the body can cheat. It's one of the toughest and most effective abdominal exercises you'll ever find.

1 Lie on your back, with your knees into your chest and arms reaching behind you, in line with your ears. Keep the ribcage anchored and belly scooped. Breathe in to prepare, with the spine long and relaxed.

2 As you breathe out, extend your legs out at 45°, squeezing the thighs into Pilates stance. Deepen the scoop of the belly as the legs lengthen. Release your lower spine into the mat. Breathe in, keeping the ribs soft.

3 Breathe out to curl the spine off the mat, bone by bone. Keep your shoulders relaxed as your fingers reach to the feet. Pull the belly further into the spine as you curl up towards the legs. Keep the legs high.

Careful! Make sure you control the movement upwards: avoid using momentum and dragging your body up carelessly. Use the out breath and strong abdominals.

4 Keep the legs perfectly still as you reach with the arms parallel to the thighs. Breathe in. Maintain the height of the legs as you slowly lower the spine down, with control. Repeat 3 times.

Help! If you need to build up your strength, practise this with your feet against a wall to become familiar with the movement.

Imagine Think of your legs suspended towards the ceiling by a crane, staying lifted as you lower the spine down to the mat. Keep the abdominals working.

Make it easier

Return to the Teaser Preparation exercises (see pp.124–125) to build up your strength for the Teaser series. Or bend the knees and allow the legs to soften, lessening the load that your centre needs to lift. Stay strong and controlled.

Walk the hands up the back of your thighs if you need to, to guide you through the movement while you build up your strength.

Teaser 2

Strengthen Stomach and Spine • **Practise** Centring

Building on Teaser 1 (see pp.170–171), here we challenge the lower abdominals by lowering the legs with control while keeping the upper body lifted, firm, and stable.

1 Start by lying on your mat as for Teaser 1. If you are flowing directly from Teaser 1, move straight to Step 3 from the final position of Teaser 1.

2 Deepen the scoop of the belly and extend the legs to 45°, keeping the spine stable. Continue to reach through the arms and stay anchored in the ribcage.

Imagine Your legs are light as a feather and you are easily lifting them from your centre.

3 Breathe out and use your abdominals to curl up smoothly and create a "V" shape with your body, reaching your fingers towards the toes. Draw in deeply to your powerhouse, lengthening your waist and keeping the legs connected in Pilates stance. Find your balance.

Tip Keep the shoulders relaxed and away from the ears.

4 Keeping the upper body absolutely still, lower and lift the legs 3–5 times. Breathe in to lower and out to lift. Initiate the movement from your lower abdominals and inner thighs; try to soften the front of your legs and avoid them tensing. Slowly roll down to the start position to finish.

Help! If you find it hard to lower your legs while they are straight, practise with soft knees, keeping your toes higher than your knees.

Teaser 3

Strengthen Stomach and Inner Thighs
Practise Flowing Movement

Teaser 1 (see pp.170–171) works the upper body and Teaser 2 (see pp.172–173) the legs. Teaser 3 combines the two movements in one workout – an unbeatable combo for flat abs and toned thighs.

1 Lie flat on your back with your arms overhead and legs outstretched in front. Bring your legs into Pilates stance: heels together, toes apart. Tighten the corset of core muscles to bring your ribcage down towards your hips and release the lower back towards the mat. Breathe in to prepare.

2 Breathe out, floating your arms above you. Simultaneously bring your legs up into the air, creating a "V" shape with your body. Balance on your sitting bones, reaching your fingertips towards your feet.

3 Keeping the spine and waist long, breathe in and reach the arms above the head in line with your ears. Reach tall with the crown of your head. Stay strong and don't allow your body to crumple.

Imagine Act like you are a Jack-in-the-box, springing up easily and quickly. Then slowly lower your body down.

4 Breathe out, lowering the body and legs down slowly, with control. Breathe in and momentarily pause, keeping your powerhouse active. Breathing out, spring straight back up into the "V". Repeat 5 times.

Careful! Make sure the back doesn't arch as you take the arms above the head. Keep the ribcage down and tailbone curled beneath you.

Rocking

Strengthen Back • **Practise** Concentration

This exercise is the counterpose to the Teaser series, as it takes your spine into the opposite movement to stretch out and balance the body. It's a perfect way to end your abdominal workout.

1 Lie face down on your mat with your legs in parallel. Bend your knees and take hold of your ankles. Connect your shoulders into your back and lengthen your neck. Lift your head slightly to gaze forwards.

2 Extend the upper spine. Look forwards. Begin to stretch the spine up into an arc by pressing the ankles into the hands. Lift the chest up and forwards. Engage your buttocks and lift the thighs so your spine is arched.

3 Start to rock forwards and backwards, breathing naturally. Gradually build up the movement until you're rocking as far as you can with control, from rib to hip. Rock up to 10 times. Release the feet and legs to the mat. Bend your knees and press your bottom towards your heels into the Child's Pose (see p.17), reaching the arms forwards and resting the head on the floor to stretch the spine.

Tip Feel that your abdominals are creating a controlled arc of the spine so that the front of your body can roll without any jerkiness.

Take care...

Make sure the arms pull evenly. You need to have even pressure on each foot to keep the rocking centred.

Do not compress the lower back. The spine should have an even curve, with the upper back opening as much as the lower back. Move the spine and limbs as one flowing unit. Set the movement going and it should feel as if the movement could continue effortlessly, like a swinging pendulum.

What not to do

15-Minute Sequence

1 The Hundred
pp.144–145

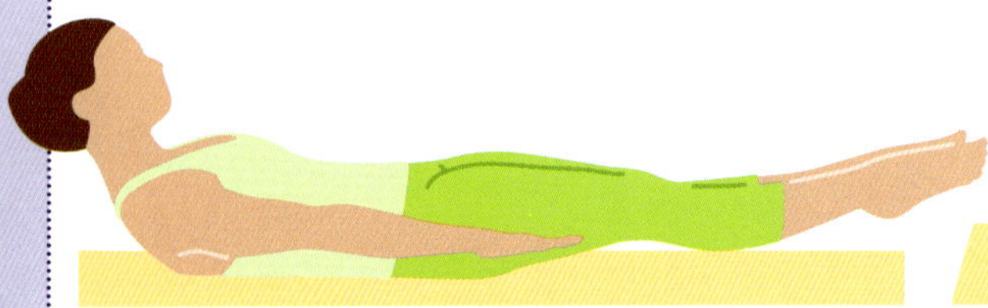

2 Roll Over
pp.146–147

5 Seal
pp.158–159

6 Saw
pp.162–163

9 Teaser 1
pp.170–171

10 Rocking
pp.176–177

3 Double Straight Leg Stretch
pp.152–153

4 Criss-cross
p.154

7 Swan
pp.164–165

8 Double Leg Kick
pp.166–167

30-Minute Sequence

1 The Hundred
pp.144–145

2 Roll Over
pp.146–147

3 Climb a Tree
pp.148–149

7 Open Leg Rocker
pp.156–157

8 Corkscrew
pp.160–161

9 Seal
pp.158–159

13 Teaser 1
pp.170–171

14 Teaser 2
pp.172–173

15 Rocking
pp.176–177

4 **Double Straight Leg Stretch**
pp.152–153

5 **Criss-cross**
p.154

6 **Spine Stretch Forwards 3**
p.155

10 **Saw**
pp.162–163

11 **Swan**
pp.164–165

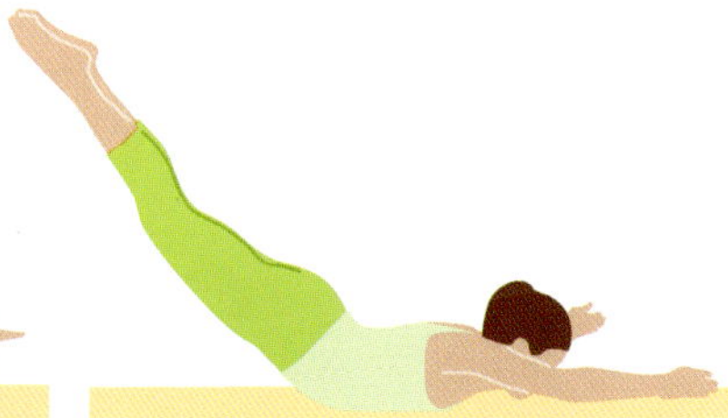

12 **Double Leg Kick**
pp.166–167

16 **Footwork 1**
p.150

45-Minute Sequence

1 The Hundred
pp.144–145

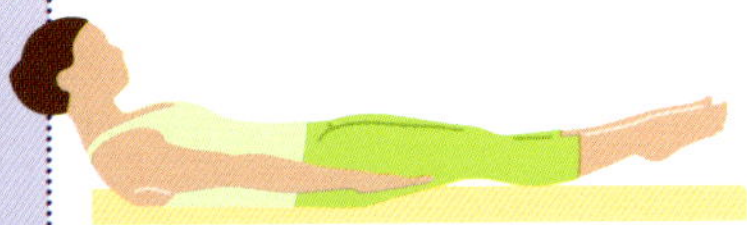

2 Roll Over
pp.146–147

3 Climb a Tree
pp.148–149

7 Spine Stretch Forwards 3
p.155

8 Open Leg Rocker
pp.156–157

9 Corkscrew
pp.160–161

13 Double Leg Kick
pp.166–167

14 Scissors
pp.168–169

15 Teaser 1
pp.170–171

19 Footwork 2
p.151

4 **Single Leg Stretch 2**
p.100

5 **Double Straight Leg Stretch**
pp.152–153

6 **Criss-cross**
p.154

10 **Seal**
pp.158–159

11 **Saw**
pp.162–163

12 **Swan**
pp.164–165

16 **Teaser 2**
pp.172–173

17 **Teaser 3**
pp.174–175

18 **Rocking**
pp.176–177

Assess your progress

How did you progress over the last six weeks? Go back and check your baselines (see pp.142–143). How do you feel compared to the first time that you performed the exercises? Did you notice an improvement? If so, well done! Keep at it!

Common problems

Did you make less progress than you'd hoped? Don't be disheartened. The challenges in this final section represent some of the most difficult and intense mat exercises in the Pilates repertoire. It can take people years to master them. They constantly offer more challenges, even if you have practised for decades. This is the beauty of Pilates – there are always aspects to improve. If you truly take Pilates into your life, you will feel inspired and awed by the continuing challenge. Remember to review principles and key techniques as you exercise. If you are having difficulty, study the method and it will benefit your practice. Here are some common problems that you might face at this stage.

"I'm not enjoying this level; I feel 'stuck' and it's too difficult."

Pilates is tough! Try not to lose focus. If you're finding it hard to link many challenging exercises, mix and match the levels. Replace the exercises you're particularly struggling with in your workout by taking a few similar exercises from the Start Simple (see pp.26–87) and Build On It (see pp.88–139) chapters. That way, you will continue to build strength while working within your comfort zone. Aim to extend beyond your comfort zone ultimately, but take it slowly, introducing one or two extra exercises at a time. It will be easier to sustain your exercise programme in the long term, if you link exercises from each level of the book in a balanced programme that you feel suitably challenges your body.

"I'm disappointed because I don't have the body I wanted by this stage."

Perhaps your expectations were unrealistic. Pilates is wonderful for body conditioning, making you feel energized, toned, and inspired. However, if losing weight was your main aim, think about also modifying your diet and incorporating more cardiovascular exercise into your Pilates workout schedule. Monitor yourself to see how your body is changing to give yourself some encouragement. Measure the waist, upper arms, and upper thighs. After six weeks, measure them again. You might not have lost weight, but you should certainly have lost some inches and your appearance should be dramatically enhanced by a greater muscle tone and definition.

"I find the Hundred impossible and not at all fun!"

You're not the only one! Often there are groans when I teach this in class. It's a shame, since it can be a beautifully light and controlled exercise and is very effective at warming up the body and combining all Pilates principles (see pp.8–11). If your focus is not right, it can be laboured, strained, and heavy. When attempting the Hundred, or any exercise that you find difficult, change your mindset. Instead of dreading it, be excited about the challenge. Think about bringing lightness and ease to the exercise. Imagine the head being gently lifted and the legs suspended lightly, rather than hanging from your pelvis. Your breathing is strong and even; the arms beat swiftly and fluidly, without rocking the spine and causing tension. Change your mental approach and you'll soon begin to love the Hundred!

Assess your achievement

Didn't achieve your goals? Don't lose your inspiration. Celebrate every achievement as you practise, for example being able to lift up smoothly into a Teaser 2 (see pp.172–173) or to roll your spine with more control in Roll Over (see pp.146–147). Small achievements accumulate – soon you'll be continually setting yourself new goals for the future.

Challenging exercises

Here is a plan to help you during your workouts over the next six weeks. At the end of the six weeks, look back over these goals and assess how you have progressed.

Goal: Control
Corkscrew (see pp.160–61)

Goal: Centring
Scissors
(see pp.168–69)

Goal: Flexibility
Open Leg Rocker
(see pp.156–57)

Goal: Strength
Teaser 1, Teaser 2,
Teaser 3 (see pp.170–75)

Goal: Flowing Movement
Rocking (see pp.176–77)

The Future

I hope you've enjoyed this programme and feel inspired to continue with Pilates. From now on, think about your goals and what areas you want to focus on as you exercise. Mix exercises from each level to keep up your interest and challenge your muscles afresh. Good luck!

Index

D

E

F

G

H

I J

K

L

T

U

W

About the Author

Anya Hayes is a Pilates instructor based in London, and has been practising Pilates for over 10 years. Anya trained with the world-renowned Body Control Pilates in London, and is passionate about restoring her clients' natural fluid movement and bringing them greater wellbeing. In her teaching Anya always hopes to inspire her clients with the amazing benefits that Pilates presents for body and mind, for all ages and fitness levels. Anya is a member of the Body Control Pilates Association (BCPA) and The Register of Exercise Professionals (REPS). She is the author of *My Pilates Guru*, and lives in London with her husband and baby son Maurice. Find her blog at http://memoandjoepilates.wordpress.com.

Acknowledgements

Photographic Credits

Dorling Kindersley would like to thank **Peter Anderson** and **Dave King** for new photography.

Author's Acknowledgements

There are many people who deserve thanks for ensuring that this book came into existence. Firstly, to the wonderful teaching team at Body Control Pilates in London, where I trained, who are a continual source of inspiration for the never-ending learning on my own Pilates journey. To my fantastic teachers over the years, in particular Victoria Hodgson at Body Control and Deborah Henley at The Pilates Room, for encouraging me to push my own body and understanding to its limits and beyond in order to strengthen and progress. Thanks also to my lovely husband, and to my family for looking after the baby so I could write this book! Thanks to the DK editorial team for their patience and diligence in bringing the book to its completion.

Publisher's Acknowledgements

Many people helped in the making of this book. Dorling Kindersley would like to thank:

In the UK

Design assistance Vicky Read
Editorial assistance Annelise Evans, Kathryn Meeker
DK Images Claire Bowers, Freddie Marriage, Emma Shepherd, Romaine Werblow
Indexer Chris Bernstein

In India

Assistant Art Editor Tanya Mehrotra
Senior Art Editor Ranjita Bhattacharji
Design assistance Karan Chaudhary, Devan Das, Simran Kaur, Anchal Kaushal, Prashant Kumar, Ankita Mukherjee, Anamica Roy, Mahipal Singh, Vandna Sonkariya
Editors Vibha Malhotra, Kokila Manchanda
DTP Designers Rajesh Singh Adhikari, Sourabh Chhallaria, Arjinder Singh
CTS/DTP Manager Sunil Sharma